Antarctic Comrades

An American with the Russians in Antarctica

Gilbert Dewart

THE OHIO STATE UNIVERSITY PRESS
COLUMBUS

Library of Congress Cataloging-in-Publication Data

Dewart, Gilbert, 1932–
Antarctic comrades: an American with the Russians in Antarctica/
Gilbert Dewart.
    p.   cm.
ISBN 0-8142-0490-2
1. Dewart, Gilbert, 1932– . 2. Explorers—United States—Biography.
3. Sovetskaiā Antarkticheskaiā ėkspeditsiiā (1955–)
I. Title.
G875.D49A3 1989
919.8′904—dc20   89-3354
                                                                    CIP

The paper in this book meets the guidelines for permanence and
durability of the Committee on Production Guidelines for Book
Longevity of the Council on Library Resources.

Printed in the U.S.A.

9 8 7 6 5 4 3 2 1

It is not until we come far down into the full daylight of history that we find men setting out with the conscious purpose of exploring the unknown for its own sake. With those early hunters it was doubtless new ground and new game that drew them on, but they too were attracted, consciously or unconsciously, by the spirit of adventure and the unknown—so deep in the soul of man does this divine force lie, the mainspring, perhaps, of the greatest of our actions. In every part of the world and in every age it has driven men forward on the path of evolution, and as long as the human ear can hear the breaking of waves over deep sea, so long will the fascination of the unknown carry the human mind forward and upward.

—Fridtjof Nansen

Contents

Preface

It is now more than a quarter of a century since the International Geophysical Year opened a new era in Antarctic exploration. At that time the Antarctic continent was still largely unknown; maps of Antarctica published in the 1950s bear a suggestive resemblance to those early charts of colonial America in which scattered coastal features were given descriptive or personal names, but the interior was left virtually blank except for a few guesses and fancies. Today, although it contains vast areas that humans have never trodden, the "last continent" is substantially a part of the known world. The exploration of the south polar regions has moved within one generation from dependence on isolated, precarious outposts and long, broadly focused, over-snow journeys to the ability to do intensive, specialized scientific studies. Organizationally it has progressed from small expeditions limited in duration and scope to large-scale, continuing, many-faceted research programs.

Before the International Geophysical Year, Antarctic expeditions were frequently financed privately or by subscription; today they are almost invariably government funded. In the old days it was common for an expedition to be promoted, organized, and commanded by one charismatic leader who stamped his character on the whole enterprise: the explorers of the "heroic age" like Amundsen, Scott, Shackleton, Mawson, Wilkins, and Byrd. Today Antarctic research tends to be a bureaucratic, apparently faceless operation run among drifts of paperwork by committees and secretariats. However, it should

ix

never be forgotten that even now the real work is still done by individuals and small parties, and just as in those rugged, simpler days, they all have their own particular motives, talents, and dreams.

It has been my great privilege and pleasure to have taken part in the exploration of Antarctica during this exciting period of transition and achievement, and it has been my special good fortune to have served for some of that time with a Russian expedition. The story told here is mostly a personal narrative about my participation in that little-known project. I digress from time to time in order to provide geographical or historical background information, to relate important events occurring elsewhere in the Antarctic and the rest of the world, or to present major scientific results. This book is, however, essentially one man's view of a small but vital part of a great and complex human endeavor.

The period of the International Geophysical Year and the ensuing International Geophysical Cooperation was a watershed in many ways besides the sphere of polar exploration. One thinks immediately of Sputnik and the Space Age and the revolutions in geology and oceanography that were then just getting under way. The end of the 1950s and the beginning of the 1960s were pivotal not only in science, technology, and exploration, but also in politics (which inevitably impinged upon us even in the "nonpolitical" Antarctic). This was the time of the Eisenhower/Kennedy changeover in the United States and the crest of the "Khrushchev Era" in the Soviet Union, marked by momentous developments both within the U.S.S.R. and in that nation's relations with the U.S. and China. In our geographical isolation in Antarctica my companions and I were in the deceptively quiet eye of this political hurricane, perceiving it from afar through the distorting lenses of the Voice of America, Radio Moscow, and the British Broadcasting Corporation.

The Soviet expedition to East Antarctica in 1959–61 was one of several national expeditions that uneasily combined the quest for scientific knowledge with a striving for national prestige, which is nothing new. For those of us actually on the ice our remote and primitive situation was not always very different from that of polar explorers of the past. Our experience as modern pioneers from urban twentieth-century civilization in a barren, unforgiving land was a challenging blend of the old and the new and of things that are timeless. In my account I have not tried to be a completely unbiased observer, but I think that my point of view is clear enough to be easily taken into consideration. Here we are entering a hazardous arena, in which the difficult meeting of science with diplomacy often takes the center of the moving stage. Figuratively speaking, we make a trip not only to Antarctica, but also to Russia, which has created a revealing microcosm of its society in this distant outpost. It is my fervent desire that the reader can learn something of value from my intimate association with these redoubtable neighbors of ours. If to think is to exist, one can also say that to know is to survive.

A polar expedition is a time machine of sorts: its members are transported a few thousand miles in distance and many more thousand years in time back to the Pleistocene ice age, when great continental glaciers covered not only Antarctica and Greenland but also vast areas of North America and Eurasia—up to thirty percent of the earth's land surface. We see the world as it was in the past and as it presumably will be again in the future. That, indeed, is one reason for our probing this mysterious region, to find clues to the direction in which the climate of our vulnerable and changeable planet is heading.

Those of us who work in science and technology frequently complain that we are misunderstood by society in general, and especially by people in public life. We are right, certainly, but it is partly our own fault. Whether we like it or not, science and technology have become inextricably entangled with politics; today the community of scholars can exist only as an interdependent part of the larger community. If their research is supported by public funds, as most is today, either directly or indirectly, scientists must convince the public that it is worthy of such support, just as they must convince themselves that it is worthy in their own consciences. But far too few scientific workers take the trouble to explain either their own research and its implications for society, or the importance of science in general as part of our civilization, to their fellow citizens. These are vital tasks in a democracy, and only the scientists and technologists can do them. It is in their own interest and their profession's that they try, and it is their particular responsibility. I hope that this book will both contribute to and provide encouragement for an increasingly critical dialogue between scientists and the general public.

1

The White Vortex

The earth never tires,
The earth is rude, silent, incomprehensible at first,
    Nature is rude and incomprehensible at first,
Be not discouraged, keep on, there are divine things
    well enveloped,
I swear to you there are divine things more beautiful
    than words can tell.

                                —*Walt Whitman*

The letter was waiting for me in my stack of mail when I went home
from my military post for a three-day pass in the summer of 1956. It
was one of those usually unexciting circulars that go out to members
of scientific societies—in this case the American Geophysical Union
—describing government research projects and positions available.
This one was certainly different: there was a need for someone with a
background in geophysics to assemble and operate, for a year, a
seismograph station on the uninviting, uninhabited, largely unexplored Antarctic continent. I had always been intrigued by travel and
exploration. At that very time, in anticipation of my approaching
release from the army, I was seriously considering job offers from oil
companies in the East Indies and the Sahara, but the polar regions
had never particularly interested me. My heroes had been explorers

like Roy Chapman Andrews, digging dinosaur eggs out of the Gobi Desert, or John Wesley Powell, surveying the strata of the Grand Canyon. Well, they had their frontiers; maybe now there was one for me. I looked at a map of the bottom of the world—nothing was there! Even the outline of the continent was indicated only by uncertain dashes in some sectors. The imaginary bands of latitude and longitude alone caged this wilderness. That appropriately snowy whiteness on the map began to burn in my mind like the White Whale in Captain Ahab's. The emptiness that shouted "Unexplored!" was soon drawing me toward it like an irresistibly gravitating mass. I wrote back for more information, and six months later I was in the Antarctic.

My first year in the south polar regions was an initiation, a revelation, a confirmation, one of those revolutionary experiences that punctuate and summarize lives and give them new directions. Our party of twenty-seven men, civilian and naval, was landed on the Indian Ocean coast of Antarctica at the beginning of 1957; our mission was to have a new scientific station (one of many to be established by several nations in the Antarctic) constructed and in operation by the first of July, the start of the eighteen-month International Geophysical "Year" (IGY). The object of this worldwide cooperative undertaking was to carry out intensive observations of a wide range of physical phenomena in and around the earth, from the Southern Lights to the flow of glaciers, over an extended period and during a peak of solar activity.

Under the permissive but decisive leadership of Carl R. Eklund, an ornithologist who had served on Admiral Byrd's Antarctic expedition of 1940–41, our young and enthusiastic team spent a successful, sometimes adventurous, always fascinating year "on the ice," as the expression goes (but also in tunnels through the ice, on the sea, on rocks, and on penguin guano). Early in 1958 our station, which had been named for the controversial nineteenth-century explorer Charles Wilkes, was turned over to the relieving party that occupied it for the remainder of the IGY; our by-now close-knit community broke up, and we drifted home by various routes.

My work at Wilkes Station had centered on, though it was not restricted to, the three long-period seismographs that I had emplaced with rock-bolts on a solid granite outcrop near the base. These instruments had been recently developed to "tune in" to a type of seismic wave that hugs the earth's surface as it spreads out from the epicenter of the shock. These "surface waves," traveling through the crustal rocks of the earth at velocities up to three miles per second, can be used, with the help of certain mathematical manipulations, to extract basic information about the earth's outer layers. The relationship between wave frequency and velocity, which are recorded by the proper type of seismograph, enables the seismologist to estimate the crust's thickness, composition, and physical properties, data essential to our understanding of the surface of our planet, how it got the way it is, and toward what it is evolving.

Research on the seismograms I had brought back from Antarctica led me to one of the great centers of geophysical study, the Seismological Laboratory of the California Institute of Technology. The "Seismo Lab" was an exciting place to work, for there one could associate, in a remarkably informal atmosphere, with some of the foremost achievers in the field: Charles F. Richter, inventor of the earthquake magnitude scale; Hugo Benioff, whose contributions included many ingenious instruments; Beno Gutenberg, who had explored the interior of the earth from his modest office; and Frank Press, the young, new director of the lab, who had helped design my Antarctic seismograph.

At the Seismological Laboratory I soon became involved in another investigation related to wave motion through the rocks of the earth's crust, namely, the increasingly critical problem of detecting underground nuclear explosions and differentiating them from natural earthquakes. The nuclear superpowers were warily searching for some way to slow down the arms race by limiting underground testing of nuclear weapons without the possibility of cheating by either side. Into this unfamiliar and unwelcome political arena had been catapulted a previously rather ivory-tower seismological research community, which blinked its eyes at the sudden glare but was drawn inexorably by the social and scientific importance of the project. My part in the early phase of the nuclear detection program was with the field recording units, waiting in the predawn chill of the Mojave Desert for vibrations emanating from subterranean blasts at the Nevada

Test Site testing of catastrophically destructive bombs whose pre-
sumptive ultimate target was a people with whom I would soon be
sharing an ironic intimacy.

In spring 1959, one year after my return from Wilkes Station, I
attended a geological conference at the University of Arizona in Tuc-
son. Albert P. Crary was there after just returning from two years as
the senior U.S. scientist in Antarctica; he delivered an electrifying
report on the results of his wide-ranging geophysical and glaciological investigations on the huge Ross Ice Shelf—which he dryly introduced as having the distinction of being the most expensive survey of
its kind in history. After his characteristically understated address,
which revealed an extraordinary achievement in polar research,
Crary buttonholed me in the lobby and asked, "How would you like
to go south again?"

He explained that the U.S. needed a scientific representative to
spend a year with the Soviet expedition in Antarctica; the National
Science Foundation was trying to resume a promising one-to-one
exchange of personnel between the two countries that had lapsed at
the close of the IGY. I'm not sure just why—perhaps because in the
year since my return I had mercifully forgotten the bad times and
remembered the good ones, perhaps because I was ready for another
adventure, perhaps because of my long-standing curiosity about
Russia, perhaps because of the strange allure of that grim land at the
bottom of the globe—but in any event I allowed that I might be interested in such an undertaking. Bert Crary promised that I would soon
hear more about it.

Shortly after I got back on the job in California I received a phone
call from the affable, persuasive Harry Wexler, meteorologist and
Chief Scientist of our Antarctic Research Program, who gave me a
capsulized rundown on the scientist exchange project, which was
largely his own baby. Gordon Cartwright of the Weather Bureau had
spent 1957 at the Russian base Mirnyy performing meteorological
research, while a Russian meteorologist had served on the Weather
Central staff at Little America. The following year Morton J. Rubin,
also from the Weather Bureau, replaced Cartwright at Mirnyy, and a
second Soviet scientist joined the American expedition. Although the
scientific programs of the IGY were continued in 1959 as the "International Geophysical Cooperation," the bilateral personnel ex-

change with the U.S.S.R. had not been extended. Now an effort was being made to start it again, this time with workers in a different scientific field. The geophysics of the solid earth was the new area of research that had been agreed upon for the program, and my station chief at Wilkes, Carl Eklund, had recommended me for the spot. Perhaps my selection also owed something to my brief association with the Geophysical Analysis Group at MIT. GAG played a seminal role in the vacuum-tube era of the computer revolution in petroleum exploration.

After thinking over what I wanted out of another long year in the "deep freeze," I called back and told Harry that I would accept the post on one condition: if, as anticipated, the Russians made an over-snow traverse into the deep interior of the continent during the summer field season, I was to be included in the trail party. Harry assured me that a field-oriented research program for the expected traverse would be written into the exchange proposal that was being prepared for transmission to the Soviet Academy of Sciences, but he cautioned that the final decision on the members of the traverse party would have to be up to the Soviet expedition leader. That was good enough for me, and I signed on.

The Fifth Soviet Antarctic Expedition, the one I was joining, was not scheduled to leave the U.S.S.R. until the end of 1959, so I had several months to get ready. Caltech would continue to be my official employer throughout my period of service in the exchange program, and the data I collected would be brought back to the "Seismo Lab" for further research. My work with the Soviets was twofold. During the austral winter I would assist at the Mirnyy seismological observatory and continue my investigations into the structure of the earth's crustal layers, making use of the otherwise hard-to-get Soviet Antarctic seismograms. When the summer field season came I would participate in the airborne and surface geophysical traverses that fanned out from the main base at Mirnyy to determine the thickness of the great continental ice sheet and the nature of the land mass hidden beneath it. We knew that the Russians were preparing a major tractor journey to the south pole for the upcoming summer season (1959–60). The following year, when I would be on the ice with them, there would almost certainly be another long traverse, but its destination was unknown to us and perhaps not even decided yet by the Soviet expedition brass in Leningrad. As my contribution to the field operations (and, frankly, as bait) I acquired some instruments that were sure to be interesting and useful to my hosts, including a new Worden gravimeter (for measuring the relative strength of the gravitational field), which was far superior in portability and convenience of operation to anything the Russians had at the time.

When summer yellowed the California hills I began my preparations for the venture in earnest. I both endured and enjoyed two months of monastic concentration among the pines and sea spray of the Monterey Institute for Foreign Studies taking an intensive course in Russian while rooming with an émigré Russian family. After that brain-saturating experience came a lightning tour of the major centers of polar research with the men who had been chosen to be the scientific leaders at the American Antarctic stations for 1960. This involved stops at prestigious institutions from New York to Colorado to familiarize me with the various scientific disciplines included in the U.S. program. In the course of this whirlwind junket I had rollicking reunions with several of my old Wilkes buddies who were now ensconced in university or government agency positions doing teaching and research. Among my fellow travelers was a familiar voice, though I'd never met the man before: Edward Flowers, who had been at the south pole station (officially named Amundsen-Scott) when I was at Wilkes, and who had been a frequent radio caller. Ed was going to be in charge at the pole this time, and he promised to try to contact me again when I got to Mirnyy.

Back in the Golden State I had a unique opportunity to observe a genuine, red-blooded Russian firsthand. Nikita Sergeyevich Khrushchev, who had been First Secretary of the Communist Party since 1953 and Chairman since 1958, was visiting San Francisco as part of the dramatic excursion through the U.S. that culminated in the memorable meeting with President Eisenhower at Camp David. Still smarting from his chilly reception in Los Angeles and his famous exclusion from Disneyland, he was due to address the conservative Commonwealth Club. I had managed to get away from my duties in Pasadena and obtain an invitation to the affair, and after my recent studies I was eager to hear not only what he had to say, but how he said it.

The rotund chairman turned in an impressive performance. Khrushchev spoke through a brilliant interpreter, but he was such an effective pantomime, and his voice was so forceful and expressive, that his audience knew very well what he was saying even before the interpreter began his rapid-fire translation. With his folksy, peasant style, his uncannily American sense of humor, and his agile wit, it occurred to me that with a few changes in his platform Mr. K. could easily have been a real political contender in this country. In fact, I was reminded of an election rally I had attended a few years before in which another foxy grandpa with a down-home manner, Alben Barkley, then running for senator from Kentucky, magically transformed a stolid, skeptical audience into a crowd of cheering supporters. Khrushchev's words were conciliatory, and he was apparently gratified by the warmth of the response. While he may not have had the San Francisco capitalists in the palm of his stubby hand, he certainly did leave them laughing. Oddly, in his memoirs, Khrushchev does not mention this visit to the financial district, though he devotes considerable space to his talk at nearby Longshoremen's Hall.

Meanwhile I was working out a cultural export program of my own that I hoped would give my Russian hosts a sample, however biased toward my preferences, of American literature and popular music. I packed books by such classical writers as Nathaniel Hawthorne, Herman Melville, and Stephen Crane; the works of more modern authors, Ernest Hemingway, F. Scott Fitzgerald, Thomas Wolfe, Eudora Welty, Carson McCullers; science fiction by Ray Bradbury and Frederik Pohl; an anthology of current short stories; a couple of issues of the avant-garde *Evergreen Review* featuring the fashionable "Beat" literati; and a collection of American ballads. One English novelist was included: George Orwell.

There was also nonfiction by world traveler John Gunther, cartoonist Bill Mauldin, musicologist Barry Ulanov, frontier historian Walter Prescott Webb, and two foreign social critics, Alexis de Tocqueville and Milovan Djilas. I added a "reference and miscellaneous" section that contained English and English-Russian dictionaries, English and Russian grammars, a world almanac, a photographic album of American landscapes, the U.S. Navy's cruisebook on its Antarctic operations, and a complete Sunday edition of the *New York Times* (the last on the advice of my predecessor Gordon Cartwright).

For consultation on music I sought out Ralph Gleason, who was then the jazz critic of the *San Francisco Chronicle*. Mr. Gleason graciously and enthusiastically suggested a number of leading artists whose work, he thought, would be worthy representatives of America's national music to the Russians. I sampled many of these works and made my own selections of modern jazz; to these I added my favorites in folk music, blues, and early jazz. Thus, I ended up with a library that extended from Huddie Ledbetter and Josh White, through Louis Armstrong and Bix Beiderbecke, to Miles Davis and Shelley Manne.

Another question that I had to consider was how much ordinary working material I should take with me. On the basis of my talks with Gordon Cartwright and Mort Rubin, who warned me about the dearth of office supplies at the Soviet base, I decided to bring a sizable inventory of items like pencils, ballpoint pens, erasers, paper clips, notebooks, cellophane tape, and so on. In the way of permanent equipment I took the latest models of portable typewriter, manual desk calculator (electronic calculators were still on the drawing boards), tape recorder, stapling machine, and drafting instruments. A further suggestion by the previous tenants at Mirnyy was a first-aid kit, so I obtained a complete navy medic's unit, with a lot of extra Band-aids of various shapes and sizes. All these things added up to a lot more bulk and weight than I had counted on for my baggage, but my mentors assured me that I would be very glad I had them.

The organizations directly involved in the scientist exchange program were the National Academy of Sciences, which maintained official contacts with its Soviet counterpart, and the National Science Foundation, which was responsible for American research in the Antarctic. The State Department was engaged at that time in prolonged and complex negotiations over the proposed Antarctic Treaty, whose objective was to reserve the southern continent solely for peaceful and primarily scientific purposes and put all national claims to its territory in abeyance. State was very much interested in our project's diplomatic overtones. With all these high-powered organizations involved I expected to be kept pretty well informed about what was happening on the Russian side of the street, but in fact, I heard precious little, and not until November did the Soviets release enough information on their expedition's itinerary for me even to make preliminary plans to join it. The Soviet expedition was heading south in two ships, the ice-breaking freighter *Ob* and the smaller passenger carrier *Kooperatsiya*. *Kooperatsiya* was scheduled for a short stop in Capetown, South Africa, just before Christmas—her last port of call before entering Antarctic waters—and I made arrangements to meet it there. I also learned at this time that my Russian opposite number, a glaciologist named Sveneld Yevteev, would be spending the year at the main American Antarctic base at McMurdo Sound.

Since my international flight was departing from New York, I left California in time for a stopover in Washington for a few final chores and conferences, including meetings with Bert Crary and Harry Wexler and with other officials at various abbreviation-ridden headquarters—the NSF, the NAS, the IGY, and so forth. Gordon Cartwright and Mort Rubin joined me for a long, enlightening discussion of their own experiences at Mirnyy. At the State Department George Owen, who had participated in negotiating the landmark Antarctic Treaty for the United States, gave me several mimeographed copies of the document hot off the bargaining table, including Russian translations to be presented as a courtesy to my hosts. Harry Francis, who had been our mountaineering instructor when I was preparing for my first Antarctic assignment two years before and was now an executive assistant at the NSF, served as my escort and guided me skillfully through the bureaucratic crevasses of official Washington.

There was a minor contretemps at the last meeting at State. Sitting across from me at one of those round tables that were much in favor in diplomatic circles was a tweedy gentleman who had a knowing look and the bearing of a field-grade military officer. We had been perfunctorily introduced, a bit coldly, I thought, considering his genial attitude, but the name of his organization was either slurred or not mentioned at all. It didn't really have to be. As the discussion wore on, it became clear that his attendance was not especially welcome to the others at the table, and somebody always seemed to break in whenever he asked one of his searching questions. As soon as we adjourned the man from the Agency made his move and closed in on me from the right with a quick smile and a confidential wink. But a man from State and another from the NSF were running interference on that flank, and they neatly blocked the attempt of the intelligence community to make contact.

The CIA could be kept off my back, but not the Fourth Estate.

There was a fair amount of media interest in my venture, partly because of the coincidence of the Khrushchev visit and the recent signing of the controversial Antarctic Treaty. In a sense, I was "press" myself; my parents were publishing a pair of small but outspoken weekly newspapers in northern California, the *Cloverdale Reveille* and the *Geyserville Press*—and I had been writing a series of articles about the Antarctic for them. However, I was getting so frustratingly little information myself that there wasn't much I could tell any of them about the Soviet project.

I had to take care of all kinds of last-minute details in the capital city, such as picking up my issue of cold-weather clothing at the warehouse of the Arctic Institute of North America, sending cables to the *Kooperatsiya*, the South African government, and the U.S. consul in Capetown about my arrival, making air freight and hand-carry arrangements with my airline, Pan American Airways, and dealing with a deluge of requests from scientists to find out about the latest Soviet progress in their various specialties. There were also those minor matters that can make a whale of a difference. For example, Soviet electrical systems use a different voltage and AC frequency from ours, so I had to get a transformer and frequency adaptors for my electric-powered devices.

During my stay in Washington I enjoyed the unbeatable hospitality of Carl Eklund and his family. Carl was now chief of the Polar and Arctic Branch of the Army Research Office, and he was also up to his ears in the activities of numerous polar-oriented private organizations. Shortly before my departure he succeeded in mustering a thirsty band of IGY veterans for an evening of Antarctic nostalgia— at which a few old interstation rivalries inevitably flared up—and to cries of "Skoal!" and "Prosit!" I received the traditional intoxicating polar send-off.

On December 14, 1959, I left for Capetown. Most of my equipment was going by air freight on the same plane, but a cumbersome amount of gear had to be hand carried because of its value and fragility, and I was festooned with instrument cases dangling by leather straps. The flight stopped at Dakar, Roberts Field (Liberia), Accra, Leopoldville (now Kinshasa), and Johannesburg. "Leo" and "Jo'burg" were familiar to me from a vagabonding trip I had taken through Africa with a couple of companions on the way back from the Antarctic in

1958 (it actually had a rather slender scientific rationale—to collect lichens from the glaciated summit of Mt. Kilimanjaro). Those were the free-and-easy days, when one of the fringe benefits of Antarctic service was the privilege of a free hop on any U.S. Government flight that had space available, so several of us had jumped ship on the return voyage from Wilkes Station and made our own way home, with a little help from Uncle Sam. One change since then was immediately clear: things were a lot more tense.

I had hoped to make some calibration readings of the Worden gravimeter at the airports along the route (a standard geophysical procedure), but those were unsettled times, and whenever I appeared at the ramp with the suspiciously bomb-shaped device, local security officials would promptly hustle me back on the airplane. At the one terminal I did manage to enter, the radium dial on the meter kicked off a radiation counter, and I suddenly found myself with a lot of explaining to do to some excited gendarmes. At times like these the clutch of impressive-looking documents thoughtfully provided by the State Department proved invaluable.

Flying south over ocean, jungle, savanna, and desert, I had time to reflect on the evidence of revolutionary change around me, such as those nervous airport guards with their leveled submachine guns. Like a great python sloughing off its old skin, the vast continent below was writhing and straining through the process of decolonization and the emergence of political independence. My native country and its Cold War rival would be drawn as inevitably to this turbulence as the predators of the veldt are attracted by signs of turmoil in the herd. But what of the "spirit of Camp David" and the tentative détente of which my mission was a part? The dichotomy between our aspirations for peace and the reality of the world power struggle was all too palpable from the storm-swirled sky over Africa.

The picturesque seaport of Capetown was new to me, but I quickly recognized the brooding outline of Table Mountain. I enjoyed a fleeting celebrity, for the U.S. consul met me at the airport and drove me downtown to the comfortable Grand Hotel. In the lobby, among a clientele so cosmopolitan it was almost a caricature, I met another wayfaring American, Charles Fray, who had arrived on the same Pan Am flight. Fray was taking over as leader of the second half of the oceanographic cruise of the Lamont Geological Observatory research ship *Vema*, which was already in port. When he told me about the unbelievably romantic places the oceanographers were scheduled to visit—Madagascar, Ceylon, Sumatra, Bali, Samoa, Tahiti—I seriously wondered if I had chosen the right expedition—or the right career. But there was more than palm-fringed romance involved. Research vessels like the *Vema* were already unraveling the secrets of the geodynamic process of sea-floor spreading, with profound consequences for the development of geological science.

Fray invited me down to the port on Table Bay to see his ship; the converted yacht was a stylish vessel, and her crew curious and friendly. I was generously invited to remain aboard as a house guest, so this time I saved Uncle Sam some hotel bills by living on the compact research ship for a couple of days. I made myself useful by helping to adjust the expedition's marine gravimeter to the international gravity base at the University of Capetown. This operation involved moving my own Worden gravimeter, which served as the ship-to-shore link, from the harbor to the university and back several times for a series of readings. Since the expensive precision instrument was being held under a strict customs bond, a gimlet-eyed South African customs official accompanied us watchfully throughout the repetitious procedure.

Kooperatsiya was due to arrive in Table Bay on the afternoon of December 23. Her berth was only a short distance down the quay from the *Vema*'s. While I was waiting for her on the wharf that day I struck up a conversation with a loitering British sailor. By the time the Russian ship hove in sight around the breakwater I had told him about my mission, and he now evinced great interest in the slowly approaching vessel. "So, that's your Russky ship, eh? Let's see how those blokes handle her. They can build a fair ship, I'll grant that to them, but manning it—now, that's another story. They're not a seafaring nation, you know. It takes a long time to learn—you must have the sea in your blood."

When the *Kooperatsiya* drew close enough for us to make out individual sailors aboard, my acquaintance finally found something to admire about her. "Ah, you clever dog! So that's why you're signing with those Commie chaps—will you look at those women in the crew! It's not going to be so bloody cold and lonely after all, eh?"

Sure enough, there were a couple of young women diligently swab-
bing the deck; their exertions were ignored by a crowd of idle men
who lined the rail of the small white ship as she made a competent
approach to the dock that evoked a grudging word of praise from my
nautical critic. Several stiff-lipped port officials made their way deliberately toward the ship as the gangway came down, and I fell in
behind them with a mixture of curiosity, trepidation, and expectation
churning in my mind. After a meticulous examination of my documents by the South African authorities, I made my identity known to
one of the ship's officers, and he gave me an effusive greeting. We
were immediately joined by a grinning expedition member whose
English was about as rudimentary as my Russian but whose sincere
welcome was unmistakable. Without further ceremony I was taken
below decks and shown my cabin, and then escorted to the crowded
passengers' mess for the evening meal of sausage and cabbage. After
dinner the Russians held a long, argumentative powwow to make
what seemed to me extraordinarily elaborate arrangements to move
my gear aboard the next day. I returned to the *Vema* in an excited and
bemused state of mind after extending the Russians an invitation
from the American oceanographers to visit their ship.

There was very little time for international socializing, however,
and the Russians were not free just to wander down the pier. The
passengers and crew were allowed only one brief, carefully shep-
herded shopping trip to the city, and the *Kooperatsiya* weighed an-
chor the following afternoon. The *Vema* people came down to see us
off amid much waving, yelling, and snapping of photographs. Beside
them was a small group of strangers who also took a keen, though
more subdued, interest in our departure. On a scaffold nearby I
caught sight of a worker raising a clenched fist salute toward our
fluttering hammer and sickle. The sea sparkled, the port hustled, and
the city gleamed with a hilly whiteness that almost spelled "San Francisco" to me. I felt one of life's doors close and another open as once
again I embarked on a long voyage across the Southern Ocean to
Antarctica.

2

A Polar Voyage with the Russians

> One cannot be brought into close association with this great people, in prosperity or adversity, without feeling an affection for it and acquiring faith in its possibilities.
> —*Fridtjof Nansen*

The early geographers assumed that there was a continent of vast extent in the higher latitudes of the southern hemisphere, which they called *Terra Australis*. After Magellan traversed the strait that bears his name in 1520, it was thought that Tierra del Fuego was a part of this continent, and that it stretched unbroken to the south pole. Then in 1578 Sir Francis Drake's flotilla was blown far to the south after it had passed through the strait, and it became apparent that Tierra del Fuego was only an island. Drake's quasipiratical voyage around the world had for one of its purposes the discovery of the *Terra Australis*. There was speculation that it might be a civilized, productive land, that would bring profit and possibly useful military alliances to the nation reaching it first. Although Drake's enlightening mishap pushed the possible location of the presumed southern continent far into inhospitable climes, at least in the South American sector, the dream of an inhabited, fertile land at the bottom of the globe lived on for centuries and prompted several expeditions whose sponsors were motivated by thoughts of empire and power. The conquistadores and the Elizabethans were neither the first nor the last of the empire-builders to pursue an occasional will-of-the-wisp.

The first Russian expedition to the south polar regions set out in 1819, twenty years before the "American Exploring Expedition" of Lieutenant Charles Wilkes delineated the continental proportions of Antarctica. The Imperial Russian Expedition was a government-financed voyage of geographic and scientific exploration motivated in part, like that of Wilkes's, by the expansive spirit of the manifest destiny of an irresistibly growing nation. The commander was Captain Thaddeus Bellingshausen, who had two sturdy naval ships at his disposal, the *Vostok* (East) and the *Mirnyy* (Peaceful). The Russian vessels circumnavigated the Antarctic continent at high latitudes, the first time this feat had been accomplished since the great cruise of the British navigator James Cook half a century before, and they made two undisputed landfalls, Peter I Island and Alexander I Island. These were the first lands discovered south of the Antarctic circle. Russia has also claimed the honor of the discovery of the continent of Antarctica because of sightings of the Antarctic Peninsula by Bellingshausen, but the Russian commander was not so sure. In any event, there were also American and British ships, both commercial and naval, in Antarctic waters at the same time, and a sometimes rancorous three-way dispute has arisen over who actually saw a part of the giant land mass first. The really exciting thing, however, is not the chauvinistic question of technical (and accidental) priority, but the astonishing fact that intrepid explorers of three nationalities made virtually simultaneous discoveries of the elusive continent.

In one of those dramatic historical episodes that outdo fiction, Bellingshausen encountered the supposed American discoverer, Nathaniel Palmer, in February 1821 in the midst of the vast Southern Ocean and invited him aboard the *Vostok* to exchange navigational data about those treacherous waters. The veteran Russian mariner was apparently much taken with the brash young Connecticut Yankee, who had piloted his little sealing sloop *Hero* ten thousand miles from Stonington with a crew of four. At that time American hunters were sailing farther and farther south seeking fur seals because the stocks in the more accessible islands were being rapidly depleted by uncontrolled slaughter. Seal hunting was a tough, fiercely competitive, highly secretive business, and the records of voyages in those days are far from complete; the discovery of Antarctica is thus as murky as the fogs that conceal its shore. Palmer did give sketch maps of at least some of his landfalls to the admiring Captain Bellingshausen. There is no doubt that the twenty-one-year-old American skipper, who had already spent a season in the subantarctic islands as mate of another sealing vessel, fully deserved Bellingshausen's praise. One wonders what the Russian thought of Palmer's crew, which was right out of a Hollywood screenplay: a crusty old salt, a clever young inventor, a lad of sixteen years, and a black man. His assessment of the *Hero*'s deeds is summed up in his insistence on naming the Americans' recent landfall Palmer Land. This cordial meeting was a good omen, and over a century later Russian-American relations in the Antarctic were resumed on the same convivial level.

Only after World War II did Russia return to the Antarctic, this time on a commercial basis, with a formidable whaling fleet. Russian whalers came back to the Southern Ocean every year and collected valuable oceanographic and meteorological data in the course of their operations, but no effort was made to establish bases on shore. Meanwhile, modern techniques and equipment for polar exploration were being rapidly developed in the Soviet Arctic, where powerful icebreakers, long-range aircraft, and floating scientific stations were being used more and more. By the mid-fifties the tools and a cadre of experienced personnel were ready to carry out a major Soviet enterprise at the other end of the earth.

In 1954 the Soviets informed the International Council of Scientific Unions, which was doing the preliminary planning of the IGY, that they intended to participate in the grand design in a manner befitting their superpower status, with a program encompassing the full range of scientific disciplines. The following year the Russian program for Antarctic research was announced by the eminent geologist Vladimir V. Beloussov. Originally they envisioned three continental stations— at the south pole, on the coast facing the Indian Ocean, and at a point on the ice sheet midway between. This proposal was something of a shock to the U.S., which historically had considered the pole its own. Eventually, in the give-and-take of negotiations, the Soviets agreed to occupy two other "poles": the pole of relative inaccessibility (the geographic point farthest from the oceans and presumably most difficult for explorers to reach) and the south geomagnetic pole (the point at which the axis of the earth's magnetic field intersects the globe). Because the earth is not a perfect dipole magnet, the geomagnetic pole is about six hundred miles from the true magnetic pole the compass seeks. The geomagnetic pole is of great scientific importance in the physics of the upper atmosphere and the earth-sun relationship. The Russians also agreed to move their projected coastal base, which would have been near Wilkes Station, to another location several hundred miles to the west.

The schedule of Soviet logistics was similar to that of the U.S. Navy's Operation Deepfreeze, which supported U.S. Antarctic IGY projects. So while Operation Deepfreeze I was getting under way in the latter part of 1955, three Russian ships were heading south with the men and matériel for the first Soviet station in Antarctica. The Russians really went into the Antarctic "cold," unlike their American, British, Australian, French, and Norwegian IGY partners, who had abundant experience on the seventh continent. But they were very well prepared as a result of their work in the Arctic. They used two new 12,600-ton sister ships, the icebreakers *Lena* and *Ob*, which had just been launched at a Dutch shipyard the year before and rigorously tested for a season in the Arctic Ocean on the punishing Northern Sea Route, and a small refrigerator ship with the unromantic designation *Number Seven*. The expedition was led by Mikhail M. Somov, a noted polar geographer, who assumed overall charge of the Soviet Antarctic program thereafter. Somov had established "North Pole Two" in 1950, the first station on the Arctic sea ice after the Second World War (North Pole One was the pioneering Arctic drift station of Ivan Papanin in 1937–38). In another link to the heroic past, Somov's aviation section was commanded by the great polar airman Cherevichny, whose illustrious career reached back to Papanin's time.

After a few days of aerial reconnaissance, the Russian explorers found a suitable site for their first base in mid-January 1956 on a stretch of ice and rockbound shore southwest of Australia known as the Queen Mary Coast. It was not far from where a detachment of Sir Douglas Mawson's Australian expedition had endured a terrible winter in 1912, in one of the great epics of polar exploration. The Soviet wintering party of ninety-two men (a very large expedition by earlier standards) and a temporary construction crew began offloading stores and building the base, and on February 13, 1956, the station Mirnyy was officially commissioned. It was given the name of one of Bellingshausen's ships as a sign of historical continuity, but the meaning, peaceful, was also intended to be symbolic.

The Russians lost little time in getting a train of powerful tractors and ponderous sledges under way, and before winter descended the trail party, led by Somov, had constructed the well-named Pionerskaya Station, 230 miles inland at an altitude of 8850 feet. Here five men settled in for the first full winter anybody had ever spent in the interior of the Antarctic continent. In August (equivalent to February in the northern hemisphere) the Pionerskaya weather station recorded a new low temperature for Antarctica, $-67°$ C ($-88°$ F). The world's record, however, was still held by a town in Siberia, Verkhoyansk, at $-90°$ F.

In the austral spring (late in 1956) Soviet aviators ranged extensively along the coast and established a small station called Oazis in the Bunger Hills, 225 miles east of Mirnyy. This surprisingly large icefree area had been discovered by Lieutenant Commander David E. Bunger during the U.S. Navy's Antarctic reconnaissance expedition, Operation Highjump, in 1947; it had caused a great stir at the time because of the Jules Verne-like implications of a "hot spot" in frigid Antarctica, but it turned out to be a pretty grim place, more a desert than an oasis. This station was occupied for two years by the Russians and then mothballed. The Soviets made other flights farther east, including one that brought them to the vicinity of the future Wilkes Station shortly before the American task group first landed there.

The Second Soviet Antarctic Expedition under A. F. Treshnikov was even larger than the first. One hundred fifty men were brought down to winter over, and the *Kooperatsiya*, a smaller, ice-strengthened freight and passenger carrier, joined the big icebreakers *Ob* and *Lena*. While my party was frantically engaged in setting up Wilkes Station in early 1957 the Russian expedition was already striking boldly into the ice-covered hinterland in furtherance of their ambitious goal of building two scientific stations in the deep interior of the continent. Station Vostok (named for the flagship of the Bellingshausen expedition) was to be constructed at the south geomagnetic pole, some nine hundred miles south of Mirnyy. The other station, at the pole of inaccessibility, would be thirteen hundred miles across the ice sheet from the coastal headquarters.

In March the first of two tractor trains reached a point 520 miles inland and established an advance supply depot and airstrip, which was designated Komsomolskaya in honor of Komsomol, the Communist youth organization: it was not manned, and the now empty supply train returned to its base. The main Vostok party, which was to resupply at Komsomolskaya and then push on, had gone 390 miles from Mirnyy by mid-April, but it encountered such severe weather and difficult surface conditions that the Russians dug in where they were for a long, uncomfortable winter. This temporary station was called Vostok-1; the arduous march to the geomagnetic pole would be resumed at the first sign of spring. Pionerskaya was also occupied that winter, so for the start of the IGY the Russians, like the Americans (with Amundsen-Scott and Byrd) had two stations established on the inland ice, though they were considerably short of their ultimate goals. Vostok-1 just missed setting a new record for cold with a reading of −73° (−100° F); at Ed Flowers' south pole weather station the temperature dropped to −102° F.

In October 1957 the slow, laborious overland movement began again. Treshnikov led a large, heavily loaded tractor train out of Mirnyy that reached the Komsomolskaya depot and refueled and replenished its supplies there early the next month. Thereafter Komsomolskaya was manned continuously until 1959. Despite almost insuperable traveling conditions the trail party obstinately plowed on through intractably deep and soft snow to the geomagnetic pole where, on December 16, 1957, Vostok Station was finally established. Station Leader Vasily S. Sidorov and a party of eleven men were left to winter over at this remote outpost on the ice plateau 11,500 feet above sea level, and the tractor train returned to Mirnyy.

Another trail party left Mirnyy that December: it took more fuel and supplies to Vostok, then returned to Komsomolskaya and set out from there on a new heading in pursuit of the distant pole of inaccessibility. Again the going was very tough, and with the season becoming dangerously late, the party pulled up at an intermediate spot on February 16, 1958, and opened Sovietskaya Station 11,700 feet above the sea. Though this position was unplanned, it was near enough to the goal, and for the scientific purpose of studying the extreme interior of the polar ice sheet it would serve as well. Six men wintered here under the leadership of V. K. Babarykin. Sovietskaya and Vostok stations both set new world records for low temperatures that winter, the final extreme minimum being −87.4° C (−125° F) at Vostok, so the Russians could now claim the "Pole of Cold." With the three stations established on the ice plateau, plus Mirnyy, Pionerskaya, and Oazis, they now had six permanent bases in Antarctica for the second phase of the IGY in 1958. The Third Expedition, commanded by Ye. I. Tolstikov, operated this array of scientific stations.

With the end of the IGY in sight, Soviet planners were faced with the same problem as ours. Should they continue this distant and expensive operation after the big, prestigious international push was over? Their answer was, not surprisingly, similar to ours: yes, but on a more modest scale. One more dramatic move was still psychologically necessary, of course, the embarrassingly unfinished drive to the pole of inaccessibility, whose name was becoming mockingly appropriate. The long-sought objective was reached at last by a party led by Tolstikov on December 14, 1958. The site was occupied for only two weeks, until the official end of the IGY, then abandoned, though the shelters and basic equipment were left intact for future use.

With the Fourth Expedition, directed by A. G. Dralkin, the Soviet Antarctic program underwent retrenchment and a change in focus. The personnel complement was reduced from 185 to 113 men, and Sovietskaya, Pionerskaya, and Oazis were closed down in January 1959 (Oazis station was turned over to a small Polish contingent, but the Russo-Polish relationship proved acrimonious, and the Poles soon abandoned it). Komsomolskaya was converted to seasonal use as a weather station and logistical support base for air operations in the summer. On the other hand, two thousand miles to the west, on the coast of Queen Maud Land, a landing party from the *Ob* established a new permanent station which was named, with history in mind again, for M. P. Lazarev, Bellingshausen's second-in-command. Lazarev Station was intended as the base for an investigation of a nearby ice shelf and for an ambitious geological exploration program in a range of little-known mountains a short distance inland.

Russian Antarctic explorers had attained the geomagnetic pole and the pole of inaccessibility, achievements so difficult that no one else had even tried to compete with them, but they were still drawn by the historical lure of the geographic south pole. Up until 1959 only four expeditions had reached the pole overland, those of Amundsen, Scott, Hillary, and Fuchs, and these had all started from West Antarctica. There was still a magnificent exploit to be performed by reaching the glamorous pole the long way, across the high bulk of east Antarctica and, in both a geographic and a symbolic sense, linking east and west.

Early in 1959 the Russians began to set the stage systematically for an attempt on the south pole. Three powerful new over-snow cruisers, the thirty-four-ton Kharkovchankas, were driven from Mirnyy to Komsomolskaya before winter fell to be poised for the long trek in the spring. Late in September a tractor train with most of the trail party and a load of supplies and fuel aboard for the assault on the pole left Mirnyy for Komsomolskaya. More men and matériel were flown there in October, and final preparations were made. On November 6 the South Pole Traverse left Komsomolskaya and headed for Vostok with the three Kharkovchankas and two older and smaller but reconditioned Pingvin (Penguin) tractors. They reached the geomagnetic pole station on November 29, and the expedition leader, Dralkin, flew out from Mirnyy to take command of the final dash. More fuel was airlifted to the party for the oil-guzzling tractors at this time. The sixteen-man polar team left Vostok in two Kharkovchankas and one Pingvin on Decmeber 8 to cover the eight hundred miles of high, cold, lifeless plateau that separated them from the south pole. On December 26 the Soviet explorers reached their goal, the axis of the earth, after an amazingly fast run. They were cordially greeted by Ed Flowers and the American crew of Amundsen-Scott Station. After a festive three-day visit the Soviet expedition drove back to Vostok in triumph.

The exciting news of the arrival of the Russian explorers at the south pole reached us aboard the *Kooperatsiya* as she was plunging through the "roaring forties" southeast of Capetown. The Russians received the bulletin with cries of "Urrah!" slaps on the back, and rounds of handshakes. Somebody instantly produced a bottle of vodka, and we all drank toasts to the momentous achievements of the present and the even more glorious future they heralded. Nobody doubted in the least that the hands across the frozen pole marked the demise of the Cold War.

The scene of our celebration was the musical saloon, which served as a common room and auditorium for passengers. The saloon was a cheerful place with a grand piano, several large, sturdy tables, a thick though somewhat worn oriental carpet, and a colorful gas fireplace. On the elaborately carved mantel were plaster busts of Tchaikovsky and Beethoven, while on the wood-paneled wall hung a reproduction of a traditional favorite, Ilya Repin's *Cossacks Drafting a Letter to the Turkish Sultan*, and another painting with the conventional theme *Lenin Addressing the Masses*. There were stacks of dog-eared magazines lying around: *Krokodil*, the satirical and humorous journal, *Sovietsky Soyuz*, the illustrated monthly, and *Vodnyy Transport*, house organ of the maritime industry. In the passageway outside I was gratified to see, in a long row of Antarctic photographs, a shot of my friend Carl Eklund, taken during a brief visit he made to Mirnyy aboard a U.S. icebreaker at the conclusion of our year at Wilkes Station.

It was a two-week cruise across the Southern Ocean from Capetown to the vicinity of Mirnyy, and I soon settled into the shipboard routine that the other passengers had become accustomed to in the wearisome months since they had left Leningrad. We were served breakfast at 7:30, dinner at noon, afternoon tea at 3:30, and supper at 7:00. Breakfast consisted of tea, bread and butter, and either hard-boiled eggs, dried fish, or cheese; dinner might be sausage or ground beef patties and kasha (buckwheat cereal); supper was usually some kind of meat (beef, mutton, or unidentifiable) with rice or potatoes. There were also delicious appetizers and desserts like jellied meats, fruit compote, cucumber salad, and, for a short while after we left Capetown, fresh oranges and bananas from South Africa.

Each meal was followed by a *gulyanye*, the customary promenade around the decks from stem to stern, to shake down the meal. After our collective exercise we would gather in the musical saloon or the adjoining recreation room for study, writing, discussion, and such games as chess, dominoes, and ping-pong. Dominoes was the most popular parlor game, taking the place that the craze for cribbage had in the U.S. Navy at the time. Card games were rare. Wherever you went there was intermittent background music from the public-address system, punctuated by ship or expedition announcements and news broadcasts from Radio Moscow. In the evening we could watch movies or listen to lectures by expedition personnel on various branches of Antarctic research.

There was more than enough room on the *Kooperatsiya* for the forty-odd expedition members, and our accommodations were spacious and comfortable. I shared a first-class cabin with Vasily, who had been the first leader to winter over at Vostok Station and was going back there to take charge again. Our cabin was furnished with curtained bunks and generous-sized wall lockers, a desk, chairs, wash-basin, and even a rug on the deck—a far cry from the constricted, spartan quarters on the crowded icebreakers of Operation Deep-freeze.

Another difference from life aboard the American icebreakers I had traveled on was the lack of fraternization between expedition members and the crew of the *Kooperatsiya*. The social atmosphere was more like that of an ordinary passenger liner than the over-crowded but familylike *Northwind*, the Coast Guard cutter on which I had first sailed to the Antarctic. We saw little of the crew except for the squad of fifteen women who did scullery chores, cleaned our rooms, and waited on table in the dining saloon. Hardworking they surely were, but they remained feminine, too. I saw one slender maiden cross a heaving deck carrying a couple of buckets of hot water while wearing fancy high-heeled, open-toed shoes. But my British seafarer's surmise was mistaken. The women were strictly part of the ship's company, and they were not going to stay in Antarctica with us. Furthermore, they were under the polite but firm control of a matronly house mother.

As the lone American aboard, and hence a somewhat reluctant social lion, I probably had more contact with the ship's officers than most of my companions. The skipper, Captain Beloshisty, was a very hearty and friendly man, and I spent some fascinating hours on the bridge with him and the man who was taking over as chief engineer at Mirnyy, Viktor Ivanovich Venediktov, talking about the sea, ice, ice-breakers, and Venediktov's specialty, marine engines. The captain was familiar with the *Northwind* and its sister ships, the Windclass icebreakers, several of which had been lent to Russia during the Second World War. His hardy little *Kooperatsiya* was a regular on the Northern Sea route that traverses the Siberian coast during the short Arctic summer, and she had met plenty of sea ice in her long service afloat. Venediktov remembered seeing the *Kooperatsiya* for the first time from the Leningrad-Kronstadt ferry when he was a youth, and he later encountered her under less pleasant circumstances in Murmansk, when she was part of the gallant fleet that kept Russia supplied from the West in World War II.

The senior ice pilot, whose job was to help navigate the ship through the pack ice, asked me to assist in his English-language class as that pedagogical paragon, the native speaker, giving examples of American pronunciation. The class included several members of the expedition and crew, among whom, to my delight, were a couple of the crewwomen. All were very serious, determined students. The pilot-teacher was an easygoing type who turned out to be a connoisseur of gin. He was especially fond of the product of a particular distillery in South Africa, a bottle of which he had obtained in Capetown. After class he would sometimes invite me to his cabin, open his liquor locker, and share with me what to him was an exotic treat.

My first acquaintances aboard the ship were the engineer, Venediktov, and Sidorov and his group who were going to winter at Vostok, with whom I usually shared a table at dinner. These young men were understandably excited about the prospect of spending a year at the coldest place on earth, and they carried on continuous, lively conversations, but fortunately they also had the patience to explain unfamiliar Russian words and phrases to me. The Vostok geophysicist, Zarubin, had an excellent command of English, and he often helped as an interpreter when more sophisticated matters were discussed. Like most of the party, Zarubin had extensive field experience in the remoter parts of the U.S.S.R. He had been on Soviet scientific expeditions to Central Asia, and at one of the evening lecture sessions he showed us color slides of the magnificent Tien Shan Mountains, which lie along the border between the Soviet Union and China. This encouraged me to show some of my own slides of the western U.S. and U.S. operations in the Antarctic. Soon I was acquiring a wider circle of friends, including some of the people I would be working with at Mirnyy, such as Safronov and Kamenetsky of the geophysical section and Barkov of the glaciological group. Several of the men who had been on previous Antarctic expeditions, like Safronov, had known Gordon Cartwright or Mort Rubin, and they expressed great pleasure that the exchange of personnel between our nations was starting again.

Though I was very conspicuously the sole American aboard, it turned out that I was not the only foreigner. There were several other passengers who didn't look Russian (or Ukrainian, or Central Asian, and so on) to me, and indeed they were not. Before long I made the acquaintance of three East Germans and two Czechs who would also be working at Mirnyy. Gunter Skeib, head of the contingent from the German Democratic Republic, and Oldrich Kostka, the senior Czech scientist, spoke both English and Russian fluently, and they were very helpful in easing the difficulties of interlingual conversation. Skeib had previously participated in Soviet expeditions to the mountains of Central Asia and was thoroughly familiar with the Russian mode of operation.

A few days out of Capetown we experienced a severe storm, with sixty-knot westerly winds and mountainous waves. The little *Kooperatsiya* comported herself admirably, displaying a good deal more stability than fullfledged icebreakers, which are notoriously prone to pitch and roll on the open sea. Aside from the inevitable albatrosses haunting our wake, we saw little wildlife after we passed the Cape of Good Hope; I had noticed a similar dead emptiness in this region on a previous cruise across the southern Indian Ocean during the IGY. We were far out of the normal shipping lanes, and for thousands of monotonous miles we had only one encounter with other ships, when we passed a huge, somber-looking Japanese whaling fleet.

We were sailing southeast on a great-circle route, with about thirty degrees of latitude and seventy of longitude to cover before we reached the Antarctic coast. This was the Southern Ocean. It doesn't usually appear by that name on maps, where it seems merely a southern extension of the Atlantic, Pacific, and Indian oceans. Nevertheless, this great belt of water, which extends unbroken around the globe, is so distinct in its characteristics that those who are concerned or engaged with it, for science or navigation, grant it the dignity of being classed as a separate ocean.

The westerly winds that gyrate around this watery racetrack have long been notorious for their violence, hence the name *roaring forties* for the latitudes between forty and fifty degrees south (as mariners ventured farther south, they added the *howling fifties* and the *screaming sixties*). These winds help set in motion a great current of water, the *west-wind drift* or *circum-polar current*, which circles the southern hemisphere and was one of the prime objects of oceanographic investigation during the IGY. The crisscrossing of the Southern Ocean by expedition ships on their way to and from Antarctica was taken full advantage of by students of the sea.

Soviet oceanographers, working largely from the *Ob*, had recently measured the dimensions of this great mass of moving water, and found that here, between South Africa and the Antarctic coast, one cubic kilometer of water flows eastward every five seconds. This makes it the greatest of ocean currents, with twice the flow of the Gulf Stream (and one thousand times the discharge of the Amazon River). They also found that though the flow is complex, with several separate branches and countercurrents, it is not just a surface phenomenon but extends all the way to the ocean floor. Its circular motion combines with radial flow as cold, dense water from the Antarctic coasts sinks northward into the ocean depths, reaching far into the northern hemisphere, while warmer water flows southward from the equatorial regions to replace it. Cold and warm water meet in a narrow zone called the Antarctic Convergence. South of this zone, circulating waters bring up nutrients from the sea floor to support a profusion of marine life.

These were exciting times for oceanographers, as the circulation of the oceans was becoming explicable as a great hydraulic engine driven (ultimately) by gravity and the energy radiated from the sun. It was no less exciting for geophysicists trying to figure out what was going on beneath the ocean floor. At about 50° south latitude we passed over the crest of the Atlantic-Indian Ridge, part of the forty-thousand-mile long range that, it was then being realized, is a continuous feature in all the oceans. There was mounting evidence from several fields—geomagnetism, vulcanism, geothermal flux, seismology (for example, our Antarctic seismograph stations had helped define the high level of earthquake activity along these ridges)—that something of profound geological significance was going on here. Geophysicists were beginning to grasp the idea that like the deep ocean, the interior of the earth is flowing, convecting, evolving, though at tremendously slower pace. But the astonishing concept that it was here, under the oceans, in these ridges, that the action really was—the formation of new crustal material that pushes up from the depths of the earth to spread the sea floors apart and carry the continents around on giant plates—this was just at the threshold of formulation.

Christmas is not officially observed in the Soviet Union, but New Year's Eve has taken on many of its traditional festive features. There is always a gaily decorated *yolka* (fir tree). *Dyed Moroz* (Grandfather Frost) merrily dispenses gifts and good wishes, and everyone, regardless of religion or ideology, joins in the revelry, feasting, dancing, and singing. The passengers and crew of the *Kooperatsiya* were no exception, and our New Year's party served as my introduction to the splendid Russian tradition of the gala *vecher* (evening).

The festivities started around nine o'clock in the music saloon with a series of humorous skits, soliloquies, and folksongs accompanied by accordian, balalaika, and guitar. One of the young women sang a fine solo, and the German trio added a few sentimental lieder at the piano. Then came a long succession of announcements of congratulatory and well-wishing messages from various organizations, state bodies, and prominent personages in the U.S.S.R. After this we proceeded to the dining saloon, where a tempting spread of caviar, cheese, sausage, jellied meats, dried and pickled fish, salad, fruit, and bread and butter was laid out. Many toasts were raised (in Russian champagne and vodka), there was more singing, now a trifle off-key, and at the passing of the old year everybody stood up for a fervent toast to our success in 1960. Then we headed back to the music saloon and game room for more dancing and talking and, until the women disappeared as at the touch of a wand, flirting. The affair finally broke up about four in the morning, and the rest of New Year's Day was very, very quiet.

We crossed the Antarctic convergence at about 55° south, and the wildlife suddenly became much more abundant. The scavenging albatrosses were joined by swarms of varicolored Cape pigeons, black and white Antarctic petrels, and pure white snow petrels, and a few small whales were sighted from time to time. We encountered icebergs six days out of Capetown. The first ones we saw were mere ruined remnants awash in the surf, but by the time we reached the convergence we were seeing large numbers of tabular bergs, some of them quite sizable. It was in this region of the Southern Ocean that the Russians had discovered a gigantic iceberg, perhaps a record one, two years before. They had estimated it at fifty-four miles long and eighteen miles wide, a real floating island. It had been "calved" from one of the ice shelves that fringe this sector of the Antarctic coast, but when that had happened, how far it had come, or what had happened to it since was not known.

Through the forties and low fifties we had been oppressed by the typically dull, gray, overcast weather that I remembered so well from previous cruises at these latitudes, but after we crossed the convergence the sky progressively cleared, and soon the sun was shining brightly throughout the long days of the southern summer. It became quite nippy on deck, with a stiff breeze breaking the tops of the great swells into white caps and the temperature of both air and sea hovering just above freezing point. *Kooperatsiya* was now part of the Antarctic meteorological network as a mobile weather station, and a group of observers that included the Germans and Czechs worked in relays to record atmospheric and ocean surface data every three hours for transmission to Weather Central, which was now at the U.S. base at McMurdo Sound.

On January 4 we crossed the sixtieth parallel at about 60° east longitude. Since this is the latitude of Leningrad, albeit in a different hemisphere, the large company of Leningraders present celebrated with a party, to which I was graciously invited. I found over time that it takes less excuse or encouragement than an imaginary line on the globe for Russians to stage a party. We were having raw, gusty weather, with snow flurries and choppy seas, and the wobbling of the ship accentuated the wobbling of the party-goers, but by now we pretty well had our sea legs, even under the influence of *spirt* (spirituous liquors). *Kooperatsiya* was now entering the realm of the Antarctic ice pack, and would have to proceed cautiously from here on. Mirnyy radio was reporting difficult ice conditions in the sea around the station, and it seemed probable that we would have to wait for the more powerful *Ob* to escort us through the pack to our destination.

As time went on I was gradually learning more about our expedition and its organization. The *nachalnik*, or overall leader, was Yevgeny Sergeyevich Korotkevich, a geographer who specialized in the polar regions and who had served on the first expedition; in fact, he had been a member of the airborne party that had flown to the vicinity of Wilkes Station before Americans arrived there. His deputy was Georgi Matveychuk, who had been the meteorologist on the North Pole Three drifting station on the Arctic pack. They would be based at Mirnyy Station, where I. I. Golubenkov, another veteran of the north, was to be the local base commander. Vostok would be manned by a group of twelve, led by my friend and cabin-mate Sidorov, and Lazarev Station would have eleven men under L. I. Dubrovin.

The personnel who would work at Mirnyy this year were organized into *otryadi*, or sections, according to their scientific discipline or support function: aerology-meteorology, 14 men; glaciology, 11; geophysics, 9; geology and geography, 8; aviation, 25; land transportation, 11; communications, 8. Each of these otryadi had its own nachalnik who was responsible to the expedition leader. There were also 17 general support workers directly under the base commander Golubenkov. I was sort of a wild card in this neat setup, since I would be working in geophysics at the base and in the glaciology section in the field.

Marine transportation and logistical support for the Soviet expeditions were provided by the Northern Sea Route Administration, the Glavnoe Upravlenie Severnogo Morskogo Puti, or, in the Russian version of abbreviated bureaucratese, "Glavsevmorput" (this beauty reminded me immediately of the similar U.S. Navy acronym "Navsupforant" for Naval Support Forces, Antarctica). While this far-flung enterprise took part in the planning of the Antarctic program, it did not assume the predominant role that the U.S. Navy did in our own operations. Soviet expeditions were administered by the Academy of Sciences of the U.S.S.R., and the undisputed leader of each expedition was always a scientist, like Korotkevich. The complete program, including both the continental expeditions and the oceanographic investigations in the Southern Ocean, was referred to as the "Complex Antarctic Expeditions."

The *Ob*, with the bulk of the new expedition's personnel and supplies, was now on its way along the coast from Lazarev Station, where between December 18 and 28 the transfer of parties who would winter over had been made, 850 tons of cargo offloaded, and a group of seasonal field investigators, including most of the glaciology section, landed. The voyage from Lazarev (which lies directly south of Africa) to Mirnyy would be slow, since it had been planned that the *Ob* would stop en route at the Japanese base Showa and the Australian base Mawson, where there would be fuel caches for the flights that would bring the Lazarev summer party and its equipment to Mirnyy at the end of the field season.

Life aboard the *Kooperatsiya* continued to be routine as we ventured ever deeper into the Southern Ocean. Once a week the ship's crew was galvanized into an industrious bustle of cleaning, chipping, and painting all over the decks and superstructure. The women put clean linen on the bunks, shook out the blankets, beat the pillows and mattresses, polished the many brass fixtures, and swabbed the decks, all in addition to their daily round of dusting, sweeping, and vacuuming. I got hold of a wooden tub and an old-fashioned washboard from the shy, stolid matron of our deck, did a quick wash in it, and hung the dripping clothes up to dry in my cabin. In the evening there was a treat that we all very much appreciated—hot showers of unlimited duration.

Most of my Russian fellow passengers seemed to be very interested in talking to me; a few were rather aloof. Many of the men had been exposed to English in school and wanted to try out their ability with the language of Shakespeare (a great Russian favorite), while others who could not speak a word of English other than "peace" and "friendship" simply wanted to communicate with a real, live American and express their earnest desire for cooperation with my country. They certainly gave no signs that they had been discouraged from approaching me. I had fully expected that I would hear criticism of the U.S. defense establishment's prominent role in our Antarctic expeditions, but the Russians apparently understood that we didn't have a civilian Northern Sea route and that our only polar navigation capabilities were held by the Navy and the Coast Guard.

My hosts had not yet seen the Antarctic Treaty, and the reaction of a group of ship's officers and expedition staff when I presented the State Department draft copy was unexpected. When I said, "Here is a copy of the new Antarctic Treaty, translated into your language," they asked, "What are you giving us this document for?" To my reply that it had just been signed when I left the United States, and the Department of State sent it for me to give them with our compliments, they immediately said, "Are you afraid we might violate the provisions of the treaty?" I insisted that we were not laying down the law or anything, and that the copy was just for their information, a courtesy. They wanted to be sure that what I was doing was not an official act but a personal gesture, and I had to reiterate that nothing I was doing there was an official act. They thought that it was a strange procedure and quite irregular but thanked me anyway.

Their defensive attitude became more familiar to me later. The American bearing gifts was genuinely suspicious to the Russians, for this obviously important document that I had just popped out of my jacket pocket did not come down through official channels as such things normally would. I was also to discover that Russians have a fetish about documents (*bumagi*), and when people start waving papers around it usually means that they are demanding something. This was not the last time that my informal American style would mystify them.

We entered the pack on the fifth of January. At first there was just brash—small floating fragments of ice—then scattered small floes brushed against our hull. At length we were tangled in an increasingly dense concentration of hard, thick floes up to a hundred meters across. The *Kooperatsiya* reduced speed to one-quarter ahead and nudged her way carefully through the sea ice. We saw a few Weddell seals reclining on snow-covered floes and spotted our first Adelie penguins bobbing over the ice hummocks. Overhead multitudes of elegant snow petrels formed a shimmering cloud around the ship.

The Antarctic pack ice varies enormously with the seasons. We were penetrating it during the early summer of the southern hemisphere, when melting, fragmentation, and the effects of winds and currents were reducing it to a fringe several hundred miles wide around the continent. In winter millions of square miles of the Southern Ocean are frozen to a depth of up to six feet, and the belt of pack is as much as fifteen hundred miles wide. The vast reflecting surface of the sea ice at its greatest extent, combined with the frozen continent that it surrounds, covers nearly one-seventh of the southern hemisphere and constitutes a major influence on the solar energy budget of the planet, and hence on our climate.

Late in the evening of the sixth we spied the gentle white dome of Drygalski Island rising modestly over the horizon on the port side of the ship. This put us about seventy-five miles from the coast of the continent. Shortly before midnight we were excited by what appeared at first to be land on the starboard beam but soon turned out to be only a distorted image of a distant patch of sea ice—mirages are common and often extraordinarily deceptive in these latitudes. By this time the stinging breeze had died, and the ship glided smoothly over a glassy, ice-studded sea. The sky was perfectly clear and dominated by the low-lying but brilliant sun, which was reflected on all sides by our resplendent blue and white universe. Then, suddenly, a striking white cape appeared to starboard, and we knew that this was the real continent at last. As if to confirm our discovery a lone twin-engine airplane zoomed out of the purple dusk and buzzed the ship several times. We sailed on silently through the night toward the coast.

After spending the early morning hours of January 7 meandering through a bewildering maze of icebergs and extremely thick floes, we arrived around breakfast time at the edge of a dazzling field of sea ice that stretched smoothly without a break across the eleven miles that now separated us from Mirnyy Station. A tractor party had driven out from the base and flagged a suitable natural berth for the ship in an indentation in the edge of the ice field, and *Kooperatsiya* was hurriedly moored by a long cable from her bow. Close upon the "docking" at the ice front a single-engine biplane flew out from Mirnyy and came down on the ice a few hundred meters from the vessel. Several people hopped out of the aircraft and started walking in our direction, their distant figures looking like black stick figures against the radiant whiteness. The gangway was promptly lowered, and a group of our expedition members and ship's officers rushed down to meet the advancing delegation from Mirnyy. From the deck rail I could see the two groups converge and mingle, and then the combined mob of laughing, shouting, gesticulating men came back over to the *Kooperatsiya*, funneled up the gangway and spilled onto the deck. The rest of us followed them to the music saloon for greetings, introductions, and the inevitable toasting in vodka and *champanskoe*. Our first visitors had come not only to welcome us wholeheartedly to Mirnyy and to Antarctica but also to discuss the offloading of supplies and the transfer of personnel, and a conference about these vital operations followed quickly upon the riotous reception.

Then, to work. The first order of business was to get the Vostok people and their gear ashore to be ready for the long flight to their remote station. The light biplane did ferry service the rest of the day as the Vostok party carried their own stores down to the ice and pulled them by sled over to an improvised landing strip. All this sudden activity on the ice was watched with apparent interest by an audience of south polar skuas, Antarctic petrels, and Adelie penguins that had been attracted in large numbers to this incursion in their environment. That night a strong offshore wind came up and started moving the ice against the ship, which was forced to cast off and relocate several times at temporarily safer moorings. It was obvious that the *Kooperatsiya* would have to await the arrival of the *Ob* to get much closer to the shore, but the personnel changeover was already beginning, and we were close enough to start transferring priority cargo by aircraft to Mirnyy.

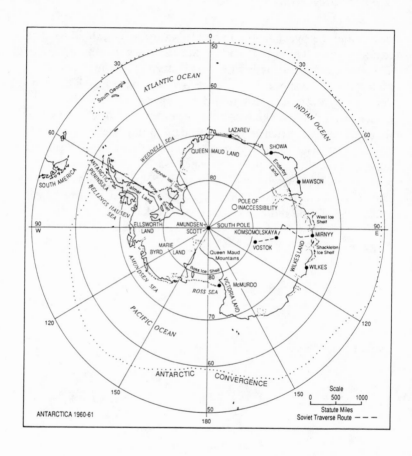

ANTARCTICA 1960-61

3

The Settlement Mirnyy

The crawling glaciers pierce me with the spears
Of their moon-freezing crystals; the bright chains
Eat with their burning cold into my bones.
— *Percy Bysshe Shelley*

You are sitting on a barrel at the back of a slowly moving steel sledge that crunches roughly over the snow, wondering, "What on earth am I doing here?"

It is about six A.M., and ahead of you is a twelve-hour day of unloading fifty-five-gallon fuel drums from the big tractor-drawn sledges and stacking them in the shelterless outdoor supply depots on the perimeter of the base. The low, weak sun is hidden behind gray clouds, and the wind swirling around the tractor train picks up the powdery snow and lashes it viciously against your face, but you are still drowsy. The men hunched beside you on the sledge, none of whom speaks your language, are similarly silent, huddled into their dark, shapeless parkas, perhaps musing, like you, about what vagrant currents of life brought them to this place at this time.

You slip easily into reverie, and your mind drifts back a few years, lulled by the monotonous clanking of the diesel engine behind your back. You are still on top of some kind of moving vehicle, but now it's

35

a water tank truck that your legs are straddling; the men beside you speak a strange tongue, but now it's an archaic French dialect. The air has become mercifully warm and humid, and mist is rising through the saw grass and cypress boughs and Spanish moss. Ahead is a twelve-hour day, at the very least, of toting a heavy drilling pump through the sucking black mud and jutting cypress knees of the Louisiana bayou country. As we pass a dimly lit cabin one of the crew smiles and points to the shadowy interior, where a coolly clad girl is at work over an ironing board.

"Flat tire!" someone yells.

The truck lurches to a halt and Camille, the drilling boss, jumps from the cab onto the dirt road to look at the wheels. The gang starts whistling and roaring with laughter, while a pair of dark eyes peers out, startled, through the sagging doorway. Camille curses at us, climbs back behind the steering wheel, slams the door angrily, and guns the motor. The truck sways down the rutted lane and the guffaws, jeers, and whistles die away.

You wake up suddenly from your daydreaming when a companion thumps your shoulder and a broad Slavic face appears, framed by a parka hood. He mutters, "Vot sklad" (Here's the dump), and we tumble off the sledge into the snow and start preparing a bed of boards for the heavy drums marked *toplivo* (fuel) and *benzin* (gasoline) in Cyrillic block letters. When the floor of the depot is laid we begin rolling the barrels onto it from the back of the sledge, our straining muscles quickly losing their morning numbness.

This was how much of my first month at Mirnyy Station was spent, unloading the ships, building the depots, and storing the expedition's fuel and supplies in them. I sometimes indulged in fantasy during those fatiguing days about my somewhat similar experience on an oil exploration crew in the Mississippi delta, for here, as there, I had to learn quickly the essential words of physical labor in another language—something for which my crash course in polite Russian had not prepared me. Waiting in the quarter-boat galley on those warm, dewy mornings on the Bayou des Allemands for the cook to hand me an outsize mug of strong, black, chicory-laced coffee, I would pick up the words "la machine bleue" from the hubbub of patois, and even my bones would know that in another hour's time my shoulder would be bent under one end of a pipe from the middle of which hung a big, blue brute of a pump. Now I had to learn words like "Ruki, ruki! Nogi, nogi! Chut, chut!" (Watch your hands! Your feet! Hurry up!) as the five hundred-pound steel cylinders came bouncing crazily off the fuel sledge into my arms.

The first work party I joined was formed the day after the *Kooperatsiya*'s arrival at the ice edge. After taking the impatient Vostok party and its gear ashore, the single-engine biplane (I had learned that it was a model AN-2, designed for short takeoffs and landings in rugged conditions) began ferrying perishable food (purchased in South Africa) and other supplies to the station: pineapples, oranges, apples, vegetables, potatoes. The Germans, Czechs, and I, plus five or six Russians, volunteered to haul the cargo across the ice to the airplane. Naturally, our group was immediate christened the "Mezhdunarodnaya Brigada" (international brigade). After the ship's cranes had lowered the crates of produce to the ice we would load up a wooden sled with about fifteen hundred pounds of freight, and with three men pulling in harness from the front as a troika and the rest pushing at the rear and sides, we would move it over the melting, cracking ice to the frequently shifting loading zone.

That evening the Vostok people were being given a farewell dinner party at one of the houses in Mirnyy, and Skeib, Kostka, and I were invited to attend it and have our first look at the base. The AN-2 flew us across the fringing belt of sea ice in a few minutes, and after circling the station at low altitude a couple of times for our benefit, the pilot brought the ski-plane in for a perfect landing on the compacted snow runway of "Mirnyy Aerodrome." We climbed into a military-type personnel carrier and clattered into the settlement, while one of our hosts hoarsely called our attention to the local "tourist attractions." The base was constructed on the landward side of a rocky hill that overlooked the shore: the solid wooden buildings, double-walled for insulation, were flat-roofed and single-storied. In front of the administration building (called by the local wags the Pentagon) were a wooden pillar surmounted by a plaster bust of Lenin, a huge red banner of welcome, and two tall flagpoles of equal height; atop one was the red and gold flag of the Union of Soviet Socialist Republics, and on the other, to my surprise and gratification, floated the Stars and Stripes.

The going-away party for Sidorov and his companions was more of an authentic Russian polar *vecher* than the formal New Year's celebration or even the Leningraders' party aboard the ship. In this case it was an all-male group, so the carousing, storytelling, and singing were less inhibited. More liquor was also available, including champagne, cognac, vodka, wine, and a potent beverage, *samogon* (literally, "self-burning"), which consisted of straight raw alcohol lightly diluted with fruit juice. It is traditional among *polyarniki* (polar workers) that the percentage of alcohol in this throat-burning potion be equal to the latitude of the place where it is drunk, which for Mirnyy would make it about 130 proof.

Russians wisely never drink without eating (unless they're trying to prove something), and the food at this shindig was even more sumptuous than at the shipboard banquets: crabmeat (export quality), liver paste, caviar (both black and red), pickled herring, sausage, cheese, bread (black and white), fruit, tomatoes, giant dill pickles, and other delicacies. I was called upon to offer my first toast in Russian, and I mumbled something suitably comradely, which received a raucous applause from the exuberant company. The bacchanalia went on into the small and then not-so-small hours of the next day, but somehow my German and Czech friends and I made it back in time for the afternoon work shift.

Now that most of the passengers were ashore, the dining saloon was closed, and the few of us remaining aboard the *Kooperatsiya* for the offloading ate at the officers' mess in a cozy little compartment that had a teapot as constantly on tap as the coffeepot on American naval icebreakers. The "international brigade" turned to regularly for the next few days while the ship's crew, for a change, enjoyed R and R on the sea ice—playing football, chasing penguins, taking pictures, hiking around on the slushy surface. Of necessity our cosmopolitan stevedore gang was in the process of creating a new language, which consisted of an amalgam of Russian, Czech, German, and English; we called it "Mirnese." The weather was now warm and calm and sunny, and we could remove our shirts but still be sweating while hauling the heavily laden sled across the treacherous surface. To avoid sunburn one of the men made himself a hood out of a white sheet, with holes for eyes and mouth and a pointed peak; he promptly became known as the "Ku-Kluxer." What at Wilkes we had called the "panda effect"—circles around the eyes caused by dark glasses—was also added to our vocabulary, though when I first tried to describe the "strange, pudgy creature that lurks in the mountains of China" I think they suspected me of making some kind of crack about Mao Tse-tung, who was still a hero in the Soviet bloc.

So far our circle of spectators from the animal kingdom had caused us no concern, but suddenly there was an ominous change. Shortly after a can of rather pungent garbage had been cast overboard we were startled by the abrupt appearance of two large killer whales swimming abreast near the ship. First their noses broke the water surface with a roar, then the pair simultaneously vented spouts of fine mist, and finally their great dorsal fins sliced the waves. The big mammals seemed to be heading straight for the spot where the "brigade" was standing around the sled when their tails flashed up in the air and they dived beneath the ice. I remembered the story of Ponting, the photographer on Robert Falcon Scott's south pole expedition, and his unnerving experience with a killer whale that apparently tried to knock him off an ice floe; the meter and a half of rotten ice under our feet came uneasily to mind. Then, amost exactly where the first whales had emerged, two more (or were they the same ones?) surfaced and repeated the amazing performance. They were followed immediately by two more, also precisely side by side, as if this were some kind of cetacean review. The creatures swam close enough to splash us with the smack of their tails when they dived. Fortunately, that was all they did. They did not return to our vicinity, and though we saw many more whales around the ship that day and on other days, they were mostly the larger but more docile sei and fin whales, and none came so menacingly close to us.

Expedition leader Korotkevich arrived at Mirnyy on a flight from Lazarev on January 10. He visited the *Kooperatsiya* and cordially welcomed the foreign workers to the Soviet expedition. A reserved, scholarly man, he made a somewhat austere impression, quite different from the earthy manner of the outgoing Carl Eklund. On the fifteenth the *Ob* arrived and began breaking a channel through the sea ice toward the station. She was a formidable-looking vessel, with black hull and white superstructure and a massive icebreaker's bow. The *Kooperatsiya* was now filling up again as members of the Fourth Expedition moved aboard for the trip home. The South Pole Traverse party was flown back from Vostok at this time, but they lodged at Mirnyy for a while.

On the seventeenth a big helicopter lifted off the wide flight deck of the nearby *Ob*, skimmed over the ice like a black dragonfly, and landed beside the *Kooperatsiya*. A group of unfamiliar people filed out and came aboard. It was a delegation from our Fifth Expedition comrades who were still residing on the icebreaker and who, like us, were tiring of shipboard life. Among them were two men who would soon become good friends of mine, Oskar Krichak, head of the meteorological section, a veteran of the Second Antarctic Expedition, and a friend of Gordon Cartwright; and Vitaly Tsukernik, the associate seismologist, who would work with me on the field program of exploration seismology. With them was Andrei Kapitsa, the departing geographer-glaciologist with the Fourth Expedition, who had just returned from the South Pole Traverse. Andrei, a tall, urbane man with an excellent command of English, is the son of the famous experimental physicist and champion of scientific freedom, Petr Leonidovich Kapitsa, and has become a respected scientist in his own right. He had done most of the seismic shooting on the traverse, and had brought along some of the seismograms for Vitaly and me to examine. He also delivered a personal letter to me from Ed Flowers, postmarked "South Pole—Amundsen-Scott" and "Vostok": the first overland mail in East Antarctica. I had some presents in my dufflebag for Oskar Krichak, including a record album of the musical *Oklahoma* from Gordon Cartwright and a stack of meteorological publications from Harry Wexler. Oskar was ecstatic.

Gunter Skeib and I moved ashore on the nineteenth. I was given temporary quarters and lived out of a suitcase while Building Five, a rectangular wooden structure still surrounded by the last winter's snowdrifts, was prepared for occupancy by our field seismology group, which in addition to Vitaly and me included three men who were still at Lazarev Station with the seasonal field party. Our group was attached to the glaciology section, which was headed by Vyacheslav Ivanov, veteran of several scientific expeditions to the islands of the Arctic Ocean and the mountains of Central Asia, and something of a legend.

Most of my gear remained aboard the *Kooperatsiya* for the time being, but I installed the Worden gravimeter in a constant-temperature room under the snow for calibration. This ice-walled chamber was in an eerie complex of subterranean storage vaults called "the catacombs." The sorry condition of much of the equipment there amply demonstrated what I was already beginning to learn: the Russians showed great ingenuity in improvising repairs in the field, but the concept of preventive maintenance was utterly foreign to them. As the summer melt progressed, the temperature in the catacombs did not remain so constant. It began to "rain," and I had to keep moving the gravimeter around to avoid the shifting floodwaters.

The gravimeter was to be used, in conjunction with seismic sounding measurements, to estimate the thickness of the ice sheet that covers more than ninety percent of the Antarctic continent. This is done by utilizing the small differences in the pull of gravity due to the difference in density between the ice and the underlying rock. Gravity data are ambiguous when taken by themselves, but they can be used to extrapolate the results from seismically determined values of the depth of the ice.

Gravity prospecting has been in use since the early years of this century. In its major commercial application, a gravity survey is normally carried out in the reconnaissance stage of the search for petroleum and natural gas. Irregularities in the relatively dense basement rock underlying a sedimentary basin can often by detected by gravimetric methods. These irregularities are frequently reflected in the folding or faulting of the overlying strata, which can trap hydrocarbon deposits. A gravity anomaly indicates a promising location for the employment of more intensive prospecting techniques, such as seismic surveys.

The modern gravimeter (or gravity meter) is a triumph of the instrument maker's art. It is basically quite simple—a small weight attached to a delicate spring. When the acceleration of gravity increases because of the presence of a massive body, the downward pull of the weight increases, and the spring stretches. The distance the weight has to be moved to bring it back to its normal, or null, position is a measure of the change in gravity. That distance may be tiny, but it can be magnified through mechanical and optical systems until it is readable by an observer. The mass of a geological structure that is of interest to the prospector is insignificant in comparison to the mass of the rest of the earth, and its gravitational effect is likewise minuscule compared to the overall pull of gravity. Hence the gravimeter must be able to detect extremely small variations in gravitational attraction—as little as one one-hundred-millionth of the force of gravity at the earth's surface.

Numerous factors complicate the working of the gravimeter. The elasticity of a spring varies with temperature, so either the mechanism must be kept in a constant-temperature "oven," or a sensitive compensating device must be built in (as was the case with the instrument I was using). There is also a change in elasticity with time for any spring under tension, and this introduces a drift in the measurements that must be taken into account. The sun and the moon affect not only the ocean tides, but everything else on the earth, including the weight in a gravimeter, and this effect must be considered in the observations, as must the distortion of the gravity field caused by the flattening of the earth at its poles. So, as is often the case in science, something that is very simple in principle becomes extraordinarily complex in practice. But with the gravimeter the problems have been solved to a remarkable degree, so that the modern instrument is rugged and compact in addition to being extremely accurate, and it can be operated handily by one person in the field.

The day after my arrival I was called to the communications building, where there were radiograms expressing greetings and encouragement for me and the Soviet expedition from the National Science Foundation in Washington and the U.S. headquarters at McMurdo Sound. Communications Chief Aralov, Chief Engineer Venediktov, and I then worked out arrangements for a regular voice-radio schedule with McMurdo. I also alerted the very cooperative Aralov to calls I might be getting from Ed Flowers at the south pole.

The genial, witty Venediktov had been acting as my guide around the base, showing me where things were, explaining the Soviet operations, and introducing me to people who could help my program. He had learned his English the hard way during the war while repairing British and American merchant ships in Murmansk and had retained a lot of earthy expressions that had originated in the East End of London and the New York waterfront. My safety was clearly a major concern for him as he bird-dogged me through the mechanized bustle of the resupply operations, and he made full use of his arsenal of expletives when, over his objections, I helped to refasten a parted tractor-sledge coupling. I was to find that Venediktov was a rarity among Russians, a stickler for safety.

The changeover was now going forward with fair speed but much confusion, and to expedite matters the leadership of the two expeditions held a Joint Open Party Meeting (that is, a meeting held under the auspices of the Communist Party, but open to those who are *bezpartivny* [nonmembers]). Korotkevich and Dralkin addressed the gathering, and it was suggested, or rather announced, that the people of the Fourth Expedition, who had expected some relaxation after the rigors of their year on the ice, would do their utmost to help the Fifth get established at the base. Not everybody was happy about being volunteered in this manner. There was something like a catcall in the back of the hall, followed by a commotion and one of those "take that man's name" scenes. After the meeting came some entertainment of sorts, as a movie was shown of Chairman Khrushchev's recent trip to the U.S. The cameraman seemed to have been there primarily to cover the security arrangements, and the film left the distinct impression that the U.S. was populated largely by military policemen, marines, sheriff's deputies, and state troopers. It certainly bore no relationship to my own experience of Khrushchev's visit.

The *Ob* broke through the sea ice to the shore in front of Mirnyy the following day (January 21) and then went back and escorted *Kooperatsiya* through the icestrewn channel it had made. The ships tied up to a thick rim of landfast ice and began to unload their 1,930 metric tons of fuel and supplies. The big deck cranes hoisted cargo out of the holds and lowered it to tractor-sledge trains that had pulled up on the natural wharf. The trains ground slowly across the ice, up a narrow ramp to the shore, and then along the trails to the warehouses and supply depots where the stevedoring crews unloaded and cached the cargo. Fuel was the big item, what with the requirements of heating and electric power generation at the stations and the enormous amount of land and air travel, and transporting and storing it was a time-consuming and laborious task. Unlike the U.S. Navy's logistical operation at its McMurdo Sound port of entry, where the oil and gasoline were pumped in bulk from the tankers through huge hoses into storage tanks on shore, here it had to be transported barrel by barrel, and each barrel stacked by hand.

Our day started around five A.M., when we rolled out of the sack and made our way to the mess hall where a hearty breakfast of kasha with big gobs of butter, hard-boiled eggs, and astringently strong tea awaited us. Then we trooped groggily out to the road of compacted snow and waited in the morning cold for the arrival of one of the heavy-duty tractors hauling a steel-framed sledge loaded with twenty-five or thirty fuel drums from the *Ob*. When it came by we jumped on the sledge and rode out to one of the barrel farms to relieve the night shift, which at this time of year fortunately had only a couple of hours of semidarkness around midnight. Then we spent a long day tipping, rolling, and setting up the barrels side by side in the *sklad*. I don't know on what basis the work crews were selected; my fellow workers were all Russians from various otryadi. We became smoothly adept at catching the hurtling drums, flipping them upright, then swinging quickly around to receive the next one, and there was an athletic pleasure and team spirit in the perfection of this task that brought us a strong sense of satisfaction and physical well-being.

I did not have my full issue of Russian cold-weather clothing yet, but I was offered one of their padded work parkas and a pair of coarse trousers, and I elected to wear these garments rather than my Operation Deepfreeze clothing, since their ruggedness made them more suitable for this type of work, and though heavier and more restricting, they were warm and sturdy. The work site to which my group was assigned was a desolate spot, wide open to the harsh winds that swept down the glacier slope south of the station. The only shelter we had was a ruined wanigan, or house-sled, which the Russians call a *balok*, where we could huddle behind a partially collapsed wall if there was a break between deliveries. I couldn't help thinking of the contrast to the unloading operation at Wilkes, where the first thing the Seabees put up on the shore was a cozy Jamesway hut with a blazing space heater and perpetual hot coffee for the work force.

One thing that particularly struck me during those early days of manual labor at Mirnyy was the paucity of simple hand tools. It was paradoxical—there were plenty of tractors, airplanes, and helicopters, but hammers, screwdrivers, pliers, wrenches, chisels, and crowbars were rare, and the few available were old, worn, and rusty. There didn't seem to be any claw hammers at all, so we used a small, battered hatchet as both hammer and prying tool. What was I to think of a civilization that had not even invented the claw hammer? Portable power tools were also scarce, though Mirnyy had a well-equipped *masterskaya*, or machine shop, with plenty of heavy stationary machinery. The long delays that resulted from this lack of appropriate technology convinced me that the Russians should take to heart the old saw "For want of a nail. . . ."

When we returned to the base at day's end we were cold and tired, but there was a potent pick-me-up awaiting us. The expedition personnel were entitled to an "exposure ration" which consisted of 100 cc (nearly four fluid ounces) of vodka per day. In accordance with tradition, this medicine had to be taken standing up, cowboy style, in one burning gulp. To cut the overpowering fumes one took a strong sniff on a piece of dense, dark, aromatic *chorny khleb* (black bread) immediately after downing the fiery fluid (only sissies actually ate the bread). My companions called this demanding ceremony the "resurrection of the dead," and while I had to admit that it warmed the innards marvelously, I had to wonder how many such resurrections this mortal could survive. The evening meal that followed the libation featured vast quantities of cabbage soup, meat, potatoes, kasha, and bread, heavily buttered and washed down with tea or coffee.

Apropos of the resurrection rite, the question of drinking with the Russians was not a trivial matter. It is a very important part of their culture. Vodka (and *spirit* and *samogon*) can be an anaesthetic, a medium of exchange, a means of political protest, even a sort of religion. Your typical tippling Russian will respect a teetotaler, though probably not fully accept him, but there is no in between—you either really imbibe with them or not at all. Sipping or nursing a drink is on the same level as cheating at chess. I chose to join in the folk ways and drink with them, but since I am normally just an occasional beer and bourbon drinker, it was sometimes a bit of a trial.

The ships left Mirnyy early in February to return to the Soviet Union. During the hurried unloading operation there had been one fatal accident: a sailor from the *Kooperatsiya* fell into the drum of a power winch and was crushed to death. He was buried at the station cemetery on one of the small islands nearby. I was frankly surprised that no more serious injuries happened during this period. The standards of industrial safety that I observed were comparable to those of a fly-by-night contractor I once mixed concrete for in the Pennsylvania boondocks: practically nonexistent.

The storage of cargo that had been piled at the ice edge continued for a while, but by February 7 things had settled down enough for Vitaly Tsukernik and me to move into our permanent quarters in Building Five. My wiry, high-strung companion bustled around and made the place shipshape in no time. We would have lots of room until our coworkers arrived with their equipment from Lazarev, and the spaciousness was enhanced when our neighbors, who ran the station's photographic lab, ripped out the wall between us. Vitaly, who was something of a student of history, said not to worry about this unauthorized remodeling. We would call it the open-door policy. In a small way, I was learning how things are done in Russia. You don't ask permission for something, you just do it, slap a grandiose title on it, and get it authorized post facto. Vitaly, like me, had done undergraduate research in the sensitive field of radioactivity. I was astonished that he talked about it, but I was to learn that this opinionated perfectionist was an early practitioner of *glasnost*.

Some red tape is unavoidable, however. I had to report to the station quartermaster at a heavily barred and locked warehouse to receive the rest of my issue of winter clothes, to the accompaniment of much paper-shuffling and countersigning. It was just like the Army again, quite different from the honor system of our clothing and equipment warehouse at Wilkes.

I was given several heavy jackets and parkas, a vest and thick, coarsely woven turtleneck sweater, trousers with suspenders, long underwear, stockings, and scarf, all largely of wool, and an interesting assortment of head- and footgear. There was the traditional Russian *shapka* of leather and sheepskin, with ear flaps and brim, imitations of which have since become popular in the U.S. Even warmer was a soft, peaked sheepskin cap, which was reversible and usually black on one side and white on the other. The boots were of three types, but all of the pull-on, unlaced variety: high, leather military boots with hard soles and heels (my jibe that they were "great for heel-clicking" did not amuse); warm, thick, fur-and-leather buckled boots; and *valenki*, the thick felt boots that have been worn by the muzhik (Russian peasant) for centuries. When valenki are worn the feet are customarily wrapped in pieces of rough, heavy cloth, called *onuchi*, rather than in stockings, and the pipes and radiators in the buildings were invariably decorated with drying *onuchi*. I liked the convenience of the high pull-on boots and preferred them to the fussily laced American footwear. The fur boots and valenki were excellent for cold, dry weather, but Mirnyy has the same damp climate as Wilkes, and during the summer melt season there were the same "trench-foot" conditions that had moved us to recommend old-fashioned galoshes for use at Wilkes and other Antarctic coastal stations.

The living arrangements at the *posyolok* (settlement) Mirnyy, as it was usually designated, were quite different from those of the American bases. Instead of members of the expedition all living together in barracks and "commuting" to their workplaces, everyone lived in the building where they worked, and the population of the settlement came together only for meals and evening activities. In addition to the workspace and living areas, each building had emergency cooking facilities in case the inhabitants couldn't get to the mess hall. The Russian quarters also had a much more individualistic and homelike quality than the sterile dormitories of the American stations. The decor was Victorian with a Slavic accent, the furnishings those of a comfortable though antiquated hotel, with traditional Russian touches like oriental carpets on the walls. It was, indeed, more like a settlement or a village than an institutional station.

Usually two, three, or four men shared a room, but I had one all to myself. It was not very large, even by Antarctic standards, measuring only about six by ten feet, and it was pretty well crammed with furniture and equipment. I had a bed, desk, bookcase, table, armchair, straight-backed chair, and shelves made out of packing crates. Every cranny was stuffed with clothing, books, instruments, and other paraphernalia. It was not a room that encouraged, say, holding large parties or meetings, and I was astonished at the number of people who managed to jam into it on occasion.

The buildings were warmed by radiators filled with antifreeze, which was heated by electric coils. The electricity came from a central generating station, powered by marine diesel engines—all part of my friend Venediktov's province. In case of a power failure, emergency oil and coal space heaters had been installed in the buildings. There

were a few windows, but since the structures were covered to the roof
by snow most of the year the view was usually limited. For the same
reason, entrance to the buildings was normally through a trap door in
the roof of the vestibule. As had been the case at Wilkes until a few
blizzards taught us better, very few of the structures were connected
by enclosed passages. There was no running water, only a barrel in
the vestibule, and morning ablutions were done with a pan of this
snow water that had been warmed on the radiator. There was telephone communication throughout the base, a public-address system
with a speaker in nearly every room, and a fire alarm network.

Each house had its own latrine, of the *vostochny* (oriental) variety:
a small cabinet with a hole in the floor and a large "honey bucket"
under it. Emptying the honey buckets was an all-hands job for the
house residents. At times, when hoisting an overfull barrel out of the
latrine pit on an unseasonably warm day, I fondly remembered our
Navy plumber and his ingenious untouched-by-human-hands utility
system at Wilkes Station.

Vitaly and I didn't have much time to get used to our new home.
The glaciology chief, Ivanov, wanted to get started on our first field
project right away, and we were scheduled to fly to the huge ice shelf
west of Mirnyy around the middle of February to set up an advance
base of operations. The section would not be up to full strength until
the detachment arrived from Lazarev Station, but we could not delay
the preparations and risk being forestalled by the onslaught of winter.

4

Airborne Surveys of the Ice Shelves

Here be griffins, hydras, and chimaeras dire.
— *Medieval map legend*

Of Antarctica's 5.5 million square miles, over 600,000—more than the total area of Alaska—are taken up by ice shelves. An ice shelf forms where the continental ice sheet flows down to the coast and spreads out over the ocean instead of breaking up immediately into icebergs. It is nourished not only by the continuous movement of ice from the huge glacier covering the continental interior, but also by snowfall, accumulation of hoarfrost, and sometimes by accretion, that is, seawater's freezing to the underside. The exact proportions of these contributions to the mass of ice shelves are an important subject of study for glaciologists.

At its outer edge, the shelf periodically calves off to launch the flat-topped (tabular) icebergs that are characteristic of the Southern Ocean. (In the northern seas most icebergs are derived from glaciers that are channelled to the sea through valleys and fiords. These are commonly called *castle bergs* because of their irregular walled and towered shapes.) Each time Admiral Byrd's expeditions returned to Little America, they found that the Bay of Whales and Kainan Bay,

49

the indentations in the edge of the mighty Ross Ice Shelf near which
the base had been built, had changed their forms drastically because
of calving. Despite their impressively solid appearance, the ice barriers that bound the shelves are constantly being destroyed.

Glacier ice has been transported long distances for human use in
the past; in the nineteenth century ice from Alaska's coastal glaciers,
such as the giant Malaspina Glacier, was loaded in the insulated holds
of sailing ships and sold in San Francisco. More recently speculation
has arisen about the feasibility of transporting large tabular icebergs
from the Antarctic to arid lands, for example, the Middle East, where
they could be used as floating reservoirs. Whether or not such ambitious schemes will ever come to fruition, the formation and movement of these enormous concentrations of frozen water are of increasing interest to geographers, oceanographers, and climatologists as a
significant phase in the circulation of energy over the surface of our
planet. Much more than academic interest is involved here, for part
of the revolution in the earth sciences in recent years has been the
realization of the organic interconnectedness of nature. Ultimately,
the circulation of the earth's waters is as important to our lives as the
circulation of our own blood.

Only during the International Geophysical Year was the vast extent of the ice shelves around the perimeter of Antarctica determined.
The greatest in size are those that cover parts of the Ross and Weddell
seas in west Antarctica (the part of the continent that lies, roughly,
within the Western Hemisphere). East Antarctica does not have such
deep, ice-shrouded embayments. Mirnyy, however, is flanked by
two fairly large ice shelves that protrude bulkily into the Southern
Ocean. The stretch of partially rockbound coast between them, previously named the Wilhelm II Coast by the Germans, is called by the
Soviets the Pravda Coast; this is fair enough, I suppose, considering
the American newspaper publishers who have been honored by place
names in Antarctica, for example, Hearst Island and Sulzberger Bay.
Fifty miles to the east of Mirnyy the Shackleton Ice Shelf begins, and
130 miles to the west is the lesser known West Ice Shelf. It was to the
West Ice Shelf that our attention was first directed. The shelf extends
for about two hundred miles along the shore and is more than fifty
miles wide, with a total area of approximately twelve thousand
square miles, or larger than the state of Maryland. Three islands rise

from the sea floor under the shelf, but they are completely covered by the ice layer, so that they are manifested as ice domes ("cupolas").

The West Ice Shelf was discovered by the German Antarctic Expedition of 1901–03 led by Erich von Drygalski. Drygalski's ship, the *Gauss*, was frozen into the pack and drifted with it during the year 1902, becoming the second vessel to spend a whole winter in the Antarctic (the first, in 1898, was the Belgian ship *Belgica*, whose cosmopolitan crew included future south pole conqueror Roald Amundsen and north pole claimant Frederick Cook). While the *Gauss* was in this fix, trail parties went out over the sea ice to explore the surrounding regions. One party went south to the coast and discovered the cone of an extinct volcano twelve hundred feet high, which it named the Gaussberg. Another group traveled west and found its progress blocked by an immense ice barrier; this was the edge of the West Shelf. In later years aerial photography by Norwegian, American, and Russian expeditions outlined the dimensions of the shelf, but it remained unexplored by surface parties. The Gaussberg was visited by a detachment from Sir Douglas Mawson's expedition in 1913. En route, the Australian explorers traversed the shoreline that later was called the Pravda Coast and passed within a few miles of the site of Mirnyy Station, so this coastal strip had some history, however brief. For the most part, though, our charts were almost blank. This was still largely terra incognita.

On February 7, 1960, glaciology chief Vyacheslav Ivanov made a reconnaissance flight over the West Shelf, scouting for a suitable location for our field base of operations. He chose a site at the summit of the nearest of the ice cupolas, named Zavadovski Island (for a member of the Bellingshausen expedition). Three days later the airplane went once again to this smooth, snow-covered mound, which rises to an elevation of 200 meters (684 ft.), and a load of aviation gasoline and other supplies was cached for our use. Our full field party flew out early in the morning of the fourteenth in a ski-equipped, twin-engine LI-2 aircraft (very similar to the American DC-3). On the way we passed the Gaussberg, which, though not a very large mountain, formed a striking landmark of bare, dark rock against the otherwise endless background of white snow. Far off to the west we could make out a long, white band that brightly reflected the rays of the low-lying sun behind us—the sheer cliffs that marked the eastern edge of the great sheet of floating ice that was our goal. In front of the northward-trending margin of the ice shelf we could see an enormous cluster of icebergs with a wide assortment of shapes and sizes. It had been concentrated there by the nearly constant polar winds, which at this latitude are strong and easterly, blowing over the great embayment, called the Davis Sea, that lies between the two ice shelves. Here something extraordinary was happening. Instead of the usual calving, the shelf was actually growing from the sea as the immense flotilla of bergs, protected from breakup by the surrounding ice and low temperatures, attached itself to the barrier. This offered us an anomaly in the natural history of ice shelves, with more fascinating questions to answer.

Like a tour guide pointing out the sights of his native Leningrad, Nachalnik Ivanov gave us a running commentary on the magnificent landscape that stretched out all around us, stressing, like the university professor he was, the glaciological significance of its various features. As a polar field party leader, Ivanov was straight from Central Casting. Tall, ruggedly handsome, broad-shouldered, with an imperious manner, he was very much the take-charge type. You could also say that he was the consummate Russian, right out of the pages of Dostoyevski: often sentimental, sometimes tactless, overwhelmingly hospitable, yet with a pronounced strain of suspicion, taking a child-like delight in small pleasures while also relishing the discussion of abstruse scientific and philosophical concepts. He was fiercely loyal to his men, but he could criticize their shortcomings savagely. Ivanov enjoyed immensely telling about his adventures an an officer in the Second World War, and you had no difficulty at all picturing him as a swashbuckling soldier. One could just as well imagine him challenging another officer to a duel in the eighteenth century, leading a band of hard-bitten Cossacks across Siberia in the seventeenth century, or defying Ivan the Terrible in the sixteenth century. Their literature suggests a remarkable timelessness and persistence about the Russian character that seems to parallel the extraordinary continuity and recurring cycles—which we in the West so often fail to appreciate—of the nation's history.

We made a soft landing on a virgin snow surface at the Zavadovski cupola. This was always a physically and visually exciting experience, what with the huge white clouds blown up as the plane hit the snow, and the uneasy sensation of sinking into this less-than-solid medium. A big MI-4 helicopter, not unlike a Sikorsky "Horse," was waiting for us. It had been flown out empty except for fuel to extend its range to the cupola, and it would now be at our disposal for transportation to the widely scattered areas the glaciological party wanted to investigate. We unloaded our gear and some fuel drums from the LI-2 and proceeded to set up our *lager* (camp). The airplane then returned to Mirnyy, blowing up another snowstorm as it took off over the powdery surface.

Our preliminary observations on the shelf would entail selected gravimetric, geomagnetic, and glaciological measurements in order to obtain a general idea of the thickness of the shelf, the topography of the underlying sea floor, and the rate of snow accumulation on the shelf surface. The seismic exploration equipment we would be using had been left at Vostok Station at the end of the South Pole Traverse, and we would have to await its return for firm determinations of ice thickness and water depth. We would have to return to the shelf later anyway for remeasurement and resurvey of the snow accumulation and ice movement stakes that we planned to install on this trip to measure the shelf's nourishment from the atmosphere and its mode of deformation as it spreads seaward. When the relevant information from several different scientific disciplines was finally put together we could hope to have some idea of how the shelf is maintained, its relationship to its atmospheric and oceanic environment, and its "regime" or state of health—whether it is currently in a steady state, contracting, or expanding. The shelf's present state could tell us much about long-term trends for the Antarctic climate and the dynamic history of the great inland ice sheet, whose fluctuations have worldwide effects on the weather, ocean currents, and sea level.

On this, our first field excursion, Ivanov was handling the strictly glaciological investigations: digging pits to expose the snow layering and setting out the accumulation stakes and movement markers. Vitaly Tsukernik was making geomagnetic observations, and I was sharing the gravimetric work with Petr Bezukladnikov, an experienced field geophysicist who had brought his own gravity meter so that we could compare the instrument readings and cross-check each other's data. It was the beginning of a very rewarding professional and personal relationship. At first my Russian was still pretty rough, and since Vitaly was the only one of my companions who spoke any English, he had to do a good deal of translating. Dictionaries tend to steer clear of technical jargon.

Our helicopter pilot, Sasha, was one of the most skillful airmen I have ever flown with. His career, in its essentials, was not very different from those of some bush pilots I have known in Alaska and Canada. He got into aviation just before World War II, and during the war he flew torpedo planes over the Black Sea. After the conflict he joined Polyarnaya Aviatsiya (polar aviation), the air transport organization that serves the farther reaches of Siberia and the Soviet Arctic. When the already vast realm of Polyarnaya Aviatsiya was extended to Antarctica, Sasha had eagerly volunteered and put his great experience in winter flying at the disposal of the expedition.

The *bortmekhanik* (flight mechanic), Fedya, was a native of the Ukraine, but he lived in Kazakhstan, the immense steppe republic in the Eurasian heartland. Fedya was a free-spirited, good-humored guy who was richly conversant with the Cossack, Gypsy, and Tartar lore of his original and adopted homes. He introduced me to the Central Asian custom of adding butter to your tea (or almost any beverage or food, for that matter), deploring the fact that there was none of the "real thing" at Mirnyy—rancid mare's butter! The flight crew also included a *shturman* (navigator), Ivan, and a *bortradist* (radioman), Boris. Both were veterans of polar operations with an easy mastery of their specialties. Boris conscientiously maintained a tight communications schedule with Mirnyy on the helicopter radio.

The *palatka* (tent) we set up at Zavadovski Lager was one of the new KAPSh models, developed for use in the Arctic. It was essentially a hemisphere of light metal poles joined to a circular base and converging at the top. A canvas covering was draped over the outside, a lining suspended on the inside to provide a highly effective insulating layer of air, and a circular ground cloth pulled up and secured around the bottom of the tent. The entrance was a canvas tunnel that trapped the warm air inside the tent. The height from the ground cloth to the ventilator at the center of the roof was about six feet, but since the tent was sunk in a hole that we had dug in the snow, it offered a very low profile to the wind. We laid plywood sheets over the ground cloth and covered them with old mattresses on which we laid our sleeping bags. The *palatka* was good and warm, and there was just enough room for the eight of us to sleep if the bags were judiciously arranged. Our Siberian-style sleeping bags had double linings. The inner one was a soft, down-filled mummy bag similar to those used on Operation Deepfreeze, and the outer bag was coarsely made out of dog pelts.

The capacious cabin of the helicopter was used for both galley and mess. Our camp stove burned bottled gas and was much more convenient to operate than the gasoline pressure stoves that were in general use at that time on the American field parties in the Antarctic. Food was plentiful, though we couldn't boast of much variety: steak, noodles, bread, canned meat and fish, tea, coffee, and what seemed to be the favorite Russian condiment, chopped eggplant. I hadn't tasted any coffee since I had joined the expedition, and here it was in an interesting and delicious form, canned as a ready-mixed, very sweet syrup of coffee, milk, and sugar.

We were able to do only two days of field work before the weather closed in and we had our first real *burya* (storm). Fortunately, by that time we had completed a geophysical/glaciological profile from the Zavadovski cupola north to the outer edge of the ice shelf. At the end of the profile we made a direct measurement of the height of the shelf's upper surface above sea level by roping down to the water over a fifty-foot snow cornice. Ivanov, who was an accomplished mountaineer, supervised our rappels with gusto. Beyond lay a mysterious world of mist-shrouded icebergs and chaotically fractured sea ice inhabited by a few seals and penguins and overflown by an occasional skua or petrel. Away from the steep cliff at its margin and the crevassed hinge zone where it adjoined the continental glacier, the ice shelf presented the most monotonous landscape imaginable—an almost perfectly flat plain of snow that reached unbroken to the horizon in all directions. It was, in fact, as sheer white and utterly devoid of physical features as it appeared on our charts. Vitaly observed that in the past explorers had filled in blank spaces on the maps with previously unknown landmarks, but in the Antarctic blank spaces were filled in only with . . . more blank spaces.

The party spent the two-day storm in the tent or the helicopter, which were buffeted by snow-laden winds that accelerated by stages to the force of an *uragan* (hurricane). The tent shook violently, and the vibrating antenna and the guy wires with which we had secured the aircraft wailed loudly, while the shelf itself trembled beneath us. Outdoors we had to walk in a crouch and fight for our footing every step of the way. The sharp ice particles carried by the wind forced us to wear glasses, and these quickly became caked with ice; face masks were essential to avoid frostbite if we were outside for very long. So bad was the visibility that we had to stretch a lifeline between the tent and the helicopter, though they were only a few meters apart.

There was not much we could do but huddle around the stove, drink our tea with lots of calorie-yielding sugar, butter, and condensed milk, and talk. Russians like nothing more than swapping stories, jokes, opinions, gossip, and rumors. Fedya was a master of the *anekdot*, a long, humorous, and sometimes pointed story that often involved the gullibility, shrewdness, or rascality of human nature. Such stories frequently involved collective farmers or country bumpkins who have just arrived in the city. A typical conversation might run like this. After an outrageously funny yarn about a country yokel, Fedya would slap me on the knee and say,

"You know, Gilbert, we all had to laugh when you first came to Mirnyy."

"Why was that?"

"That marvelous suitcase you were carrying!"

"Oh, it's just a cheap cardboard case that I bought in Capetown because I needed an extra one."

"Ah, but it's exactly the kind—to the very buckles—that every newcomer to the city brings with him from the farm in Russia. Here we were, anxiously awaiting this mysterious Westerner, this rich (of course), sophisticated American, and who shows up? Cousin Vanya from the village!"

There was a lot of talk about prices and wages, and we discussed comparative prices in our respective countries. Petr remarked that we reminded him of the stories that Jack London told about men being snowed in on the Yukon and engaging in endless yarn-spinning. The difference, he added, was that they had gone north in search of gold and talked about socialism, while we had gone south on a socialist mission and were talking about money.

I knew that Jack London was a popular author in the Soviet Union, but I was taken aback at the instant recognition when I mentioned that my family lived in Sonoma County, California—they had all read "The Valley of the Moon," which is set there. When I told them I had studied their language in Monterey, some of them quickly remembered it from reading John Steinbeck's *Tortilla Flat*. But the biggest surprise came when I learned that Vitaly was a Bret Harte fan, and was quite knowledgeable about the Forty-Niners and the Mother Lode country. I found it odd, to say the least, to be in that place, with those people, discussing our situation in reference to "The Luck of Roaring Camp" and "The Outcasts of Poker Flat."

My companions were vaguely aware that there had once been a Russian settlement on the coast of California (Fort Ross), though not that it was also in Sonoma County or that there was a town nearby called Sebastopol. That last tidbid of information delighted them. When it came to former Russian settlements, Alaska tended to be viewed somewhat ruefully, as one might a desirable woman who had slipped through one's fingers long ago. Petr summed it up when he sighed, "That was our big mistake!"

After several efforts to resume work were cut short by sudden storms, we finally gave up the attempt to complete the survey and returned to Mirnyy during a short break in the weather on February 17. The prognostications from Mirnyy were for more of the same storminess, and we had too many important things to do around the base to be wasting our time gambling for clear flying weather on the shelf. There would be a flight leaving soon for Vostok, and Vitaly prepared to go up there to retrieve the seismic exploration equipment, so we postponed our next shelf trip until his return.

As it turned out, we did not go back to the ice shelf until April. During the rest of February our section was kept busy helping with the logistical chores again, preparing a tractor train for a fuel-hauling journey to Komsomolskaya Station, which was now occupied by a small party that had been flown there the previous month. The big sledges had to be repaired, and heavy L-beam steel frames for holding several tiers of fuel drums had to be mounted on them and welded together. Then we went back to the fuel depots and loaded the sledges with the barrels we had so recently brought there from the ships. The tractor train began its long pull up to the ice plateau on February 26.

Vitaly departed on the flight to Vostok on the 20th and returned on March 3 with the seismic gear and greetings from my former shipmates Sidorov and Zarubin. Now we went to work checking out and repairing the equipment. The portable seismograph system, like much of the Soviet hardware that I saw, was of varied provenance (from both eastern and western Europe), and quite up-to-date in some respects but sadly antiquated in others. The shortcomings aroused the fury of Vitaly, who was a highly competent geophysicist well acquainted with the world literature in his field. He was determined that his country must measure up technologically to the higher international standards, and poorly manufactured items from Soviet industry were acutely embarrassing to him.

Before long we had the complicated apparatus spread out all over the floor of our laboratory in Building Five. From time to time the two aerial photographers, Fedyukhin and Karpushin, whose darkroom and quarters were adjacent to ours, would drop by and commiserate with us over our frustrating labors. Our new friend Fedyukhin was a bear of a man who had been a tank gunner during the Second World War and had almost burned to death when his armored vehicle was hit by a German shell. After a long stay in the hospital he had returned to the front and joined the devastatingly effective corps of Russian snipers. Now he was shooting a camera instead in the extensive program of aerial mapping that the Soviet expedition was carrying out along their sector of the Antarctic coast. To Fedyukhin our two countries were still the old allies against fascism, and he treated me from the start as a comrade-in-arms.

On the seventh of March my voice radio schedule with McMurdo Sound was put into effect, and I would now have a conference with my compatriots every Monday while I was in residence at the base. Several of the scientific personnel at McMurdo were interested in establishing contact with their Soviet counterparts, so we worked out an informal exchange of physiology and microbiology data. For the National Science Foundation I also had to start turning in the inevitable monthly "sitreps" (situation reports) on the progress of my own undertakings and the major activities of the Soviet expedition.

In the middle of March I went to work at the earthquake observatory, which was operated by the geophysics section. The station seismologist, Boris Kamenetski, was just beginning a week-long process of calibrating and adjusting the instruments and rearranging the laboratory to his liking, and it was a good time for him to initiate me into its operation. The seismometers were mounted in a massive concrete vault constructed in a cavity that had been blasted out of the bedrock of the promontory on which Mirnyy was built. Unfortunately, the vault had become something of a sump for melt-water during the summer, and we were hard put to keep it dry during spells of warm weather. The Mirnyy seismograph station was part of the Antarctic seismological network installed during the IGY. Earthquakes had been recorded before in the Antarctic—Finn Ronne's private expedition of 1947–48 ran a seismograph station on the Antarctic Peninsula—but this was the first time that a network of standardized stations gave coverage of the entire continent and the adjacent oceanic regions and reported in to an international data-gathering and processing system.

The observatory was set off by itself to avoid the noise and vibration from the activity at the base, and much of the time Boris lived there alone, so he was glad to have my company. We were about the same age, and it turned out that we had interests besides seismology in common—we had both been wrestlers in school and were motorcycle enthusiasts. Boris also had previous experience in the polar regions, for he had spent a year on Spitsbergen, in the Arctic Ocean, where the Soviet Union has a long-standing coal-mining concession and maintains several scientific stations. His only contact with foreigners heretofore had been in football games against the neighboring Norwegians who own the islands.

Boris was in charge of the local unit of Komsomol (the Young Communist League, the preparty organization of youth from the ages of fourteen to twenty-eight) and he tended to be a bit strident in public, but I found that he was really a quite reasonable fellow. I learned something about *sambo*, the Russian form of judo, from him. *Sambo* is related to a contest common in Cossack outposts for centuries, in which the arms and upper body are largely locked and most throws are done with the legs and hips. These bouts, which were often, in the past, of a very brutal nature, with sadistic variations, served the purposes of exercise, diversion, and wagering in the cramped quarters of Siberian blockhouses during the long winters. The Russians assumed that this "martial art" originally came from the Orient via the Mongol conquerors.

The exploration geophysics group of the glaciology section arrived on March 21 from Lazarev Station: Lev Bokanenko, chief seismologist, Boris Zakhariev, drilling engineer, and Vladimir Maksakov, technician. Since disembarking from the *Ob* they had been carrying out a seismic survey (with another set of equipment) on the Lazarev Ice Shelf. Their flight to Mirnyy with the rest of the Lazarev summer field party was interrupted by a refueling stop at Mawson Station, where they were grounded for several days by bad weather. The Russians were favorably impressed by both the cordial welcome they received from the Aussies and the scientific program that was being carried out at Mawson. The festivities must have been well up to the boisterous Russian standard, since one of the party arrived with a Mohawk haircut that had been perpetrated on him by his mischievous hosts while he was in his cups.

At the end of March Ivanov gave the word that we should begin to prepare in earnest for our return to the shelf. An LI-2 was placed at our disposal this time, and we set to work installing the seismic sounding apparatus on the airplane so that we could shoot directly from it during brief stopovers at survey points. The late-season weather was frequently wretched, but it was also spotty geographically, so we were prepared to fly either to the West Ice Shelf or to the Shackleton Ice Shelf, depending on which had the more favorable flying conditions. It was a scramble situation—we were on call around the clock and had to be ready to pile into the plane and take off at a moment's notice.

As it happened, we first flew eastward, to the Shackleton Shelf. Once again we crossed another of the many paths of the Mawson expedition of 1911–14. In the course of their exploration of the Shackleton Shelf the doughty Australians had discovered two rather quaintly formed little islands, which they named Alligator Islet and Hippo Islet. Near the Alligator, a commanding landmark in all that white flatness, we made our first landing, but weather conditions were too severe for us to do any seismic work. We made several more futile attempts on both shelves when the sky cleared temporarily, but it was not until April 10 that we were able to reestablish our camp on the Zavadovski cupola. This time we erected two tents, including a larger, oblong-shaped version of the KAPSh *palatka*. The weather outlook was still gloomy. The Czech meteorologist Kostka told us that normally Mirnyy and its environs get only seven good flying days in April, "and you have already had them." But this time fortune rewarded our efforts, and we were able to make a number of flights and accomplish a lot of seismic shooting on the shelves during the remainder of the month.

When the LI-2 landed at a survey point, Boris Zakhariev and I would jump out with the drilling tools and start augering by hand to a depth of ten meters. At that depth in the shelf the snow was still only loosely compacted. Farther down it gradually congealed under pressure into an intermediate phase called *firn* and then into solid glacier ice. Meanwhile Tsukernik and Maksakov would lay out connecting cables and implant geophones (small seismometers) in the snow, and Lev Bokanenko would run checks on the whole system from the operations console aboard the aircraft. When everything was ready, Vitaly and Boris would load the bore-hole with a charge of dynamite, tamp the hole securely with snow, and call out a series of commands like this: "Tishe!" (Quiet!) "Pregotovitsya!" (Ready!) "Vzryv!" (Fire!)

The charge would then be fired electrically. The explosion produced sound waves that spread down through the layers of snow, firn, ice, water, and rock, where at each interface they were reflected back to be picked up by the geophones on the surface and converted into electrical signals that were amplified and recorded on photographic paper and magnetic tape. The photographic record gave us an on-site monitor of the progress of the operation. Later, in the laboratory, we would play back the tape with different filter and amplification settings and try to bring out the patterns of hard-to-find reflections. The arrival times of the reflections after the precisely marked instant of the shot were the raw data from which, with certain other data, we could compute the thickness of the various layers; this standard seismic exploration technique had been used in the search for petroleum since the 1920s. Here met and merged two great currents of human endeavor, two unique traditions of achievement, polar exploration and geophysical investigation.

The commencement of seismic shooting naturally led to our swapping stories about experiences in "doodlebugging," the Texas wildcatters' term for geophysical exploration. (A doodlebug was originally a dowser's forked stick.) I recalled the time a swarm of wild bees shut down my oil exploration crew in the Louisiana bayou country, and this reminded the Russians of how miserable their work was made by clouds of no-see-'ums in the Siberian marshes. We shook our heads in mutual agreement to the worldwide complaint of our profession: people don't think about our vital role as long as they can pump gas into their cars.

I had volunteered to fire the shots, but my turn would come later. Volunteers for work with explosives in the field are never lacking, since just about everybody wants a chance to set off the charges (though not necessarily to handle the dynamite!). The Russians were no exceptions. Explosives have a strangely exciting effect on the human mind. In my experience, many blasters, even old pros, seem to undergo a radical change of personality as soon as they start their work. A sense of power is induced by personal control over a potent detonating force. Once I worked with a diminutive, normally mild-mannered blaster out in the Great Basin who was so high after a job that he was a real menace. He'd swagger into the nearest barroom, pick a fight with the locals, and get his buddies into a brawl. Man's love affair with exposives seems to date back to their invention, an event that may have made a deeper impression on the human psyche than we imagine.

Our preliminary findings from the seismic and gravity measurements were that the West Ice Shelf averaged about 150 meters (500 feet) near its outer edge and became uniformly thicker toward the juncture with the continental ice sheet; the underlying ocean bottom was extremely irregular, with a surprising range of depths. A submerged fiord more than 1200 meters (4000 feet) deep was discovered only a few kilometers from our camp atop the cupola. Further exploration revealed that such chasms are common on the Antarctic continental shelf, which is already greatly depressed by the enormous weight of the ice sheet covering the continent.

Tent life in an Antarctic camp is a world apart. Necessity requires it to be pretty much the same regardless of the workers' nationality, but there is a special flavor to a Russian *lager*. This time, with the extra large *palatka*, there was plenty of room for a radio, stove, dining table, and folding chairs. In comparison with our first visit the new accommodations were *pervoklassnyy* (first class). We even had cots to spread our sleeping bags on. But boots of various descriptions were still lined up on the floor, and drying *onuchi* hanging from the tent frame. Smells of leather, tea, and harsh tobacco permeated the stuffy atmosphere, which was barely relieved by the ventilator that kept the upper half of the tent lining white with frost. Outside, blowing snow hissed by continuously, and despite its tautness the *palatka* seldom ceased shuddering in the wind.

Not everyone had such spacious quarters. When I went to visit the other tent, occupied by the support personnel, I found that rather more people had somewhat less room. A couple of the inhabitants were in the tent to greet me, and what transpired is described by the Russian expression *bez slov*—loosely translated as "no words necessary." My eyes were obviously taking in the scene, dividing the square meterage by the number of sleeping bags, and comparing with my own tent, that of the *intelligentsiya* and *nachalstvo* (leadership). My hosts clearly knew what I was thinking. The critical expression on my face indicated my opinion and even suggested a social viewpoint. Then came a smile of fellowship from one of the men, a nod of acknowledgment and agreement, a broad gesture like that of an impresario presenting his show, and finally two words: *rabochii klass* (the working class).

All in all, it was a pretty good life on the shelf. A long day's work in the cold added all the spice needed for our simple but ample rations. Never before or since have I had quite the same feeling of sheer *luks* (luxury) as when I was relaxing and warming myself in the glow of our stove in the *palatka*, thawing my hands around a big mug of strong, steaming tea. We enjoyed another kind of warmth as well, the traditional fraternity of men working together as a close-knit team, and all that goes with it; the banter and inside jokes, small talk and great debates, anecdotes and confidences. A rough democracy in the field transcends class distinctions—Captain Scott's Edwardian Englishmen no doubt understood it.

It is a strange sensation for an American, especially one who not so long before was in an anti-aircraft artillery unit scanning the skies for enemies of this same nationality, to see a plane with the hammer-and-sickle insignia flying in and think, "Here come our guys." But that is precisely how I felt when the plane returned to Zavadovski Lager after its regular checkup flight to Mirnyy. The workers of Polar Aviation were downright splendid people, whether coming in for a blind touchdown in a dead whiteout or hoisting a rousing toast at one of their tumultuous Siberian parties. The aviators had a certain savoir-faire that, I suppose, goes with the profession. André Malraux has observed that the experience of flying adds a quality of flexibility to the human mind, and I found this to be very much the case with our *letchiki* (pilots); the mental rigidity encouraged in their society was noticeably absent in them.

Our work caused some anxious moments for those responsible for our transportation. The LI-2 pilot, Yuri, was a trifle uneasy about the explosions that Vitaly and Boris were setting off so cavalierly beside his precious ship. When the blast of tamped snow came out of the shot-hole it sometimes looked as if it were going to take a propellor or the landing gear along with it. For Yuri, who like most of the flyers had served in the war, this brought back emotion-charged memories. Apparently it did for our navigator, Ivan, too. One day he confronted me and said, apropos of nothing, in broken English, something like:

"Gret False."

"I beg your pardon?"

"You know ples called Gret False?"

It dawned on me. "You mean Great Falls, Montana?"

"Da, da, Gret False. You know letchik with familia like yours, 'Stuart?' "

Ivan had worked as navigator on American lend-lease flights between the United States and Siberia during World War II. Once he had flown with a pilot named Stuart, and they had cracked up in a blizzard near Great Falls; Ivan almost lost his arm in the crash, but a brilliant American flight surgeon was able to save it. He also knew Fairbanks well, and once had gone as far as Boston to pick up a plane. I had never met his friend Stuart, but Ivan told me with much warmth of the close friendship they had during his stay in the hospital and how much he had enjoyed flying with all the American airmen he had known. He gave a vigorous thumbs-up sign and exclaimed, "Good boys!"

We left the West Ice Shelf at the end of April. The glaciology section planned to return in the spring for more intensive studies, including a closer look at the cupola, which was really a small, grounded icecap, and its complex relationship to the shelf flowing around it. Meanwhile Zavadovski Lager would be occupied by a party of meteorologists led by their section chief, Oskar Krichak. Two other outlying meteorological stations under Krichak's direction were established at about the same time: Mir (peace) on Drygalski Island in the

Davis Sea, and Pobeda (victory), on a huge, recently discovered ice island north of the Shackleton Ice Shelf. These substations were the beginning of Krichak's ambitious program of manning a network of weather observation posts throughout the polar winter.

We had made a good start in investigating the ice shelves. A lot remained to be learned—and still does to this day—about these fascinating geographical features and the mysterious seas hidden beneath them, protected from human curiosity by a shield of ice and snow hundreds of feet thick. The problems posed by these truly black seas are many and exciting. What kinds of creatures, if any, can live in the eternal darkness of these frigid, isolated waters? How does the water circulate, and to what extent is it melting away the bottom of the shelf or freezing onto it? What geological bodies and mineral deposits lie beneath the subshelf waters, and what can they tell us about Antarctica's past and, perhaps, its future? These questions, which intrigued us as we sat around the stove and talked over our tea in the *palatka* during those lengthening nights of 1960, are only now beginning to be answered, and they continue to lure explorers to these ultimate sanctums of Neptune.

5

Winter Life
at Mirnyy

After dinner a half-tankard of beer was served out to
each; at four o'clock a glass of rum punch with lemon and
sugar. After this the crew were as gay as if they had been
in Russia on a feast day, instead of being far away from
their own country in the Antarctic Ocean, surrounded by
fogs in the darkness of continual night and snow.

—*Thaddeus Bellingshausen*

As the days became shorter and the storms more frequent, we had to
spend more and more of our time indoors. Life at Mirnyy revolved
around the *kayut kompaniya* (dining hall), which also served as a
conference room, recreation area, auditorium, and movie theater. It
was a spacious room with a number of small tables and chairs scattered about, and alcoves with built-in benches along the walls. There
was not much in the way of decoration aside from the large portraits
of Khrushchev and Lenin hanging in conspicuous positions. The
well-equipped kitchen was at the rear, behind a short serving counter,
and still farther back was a large, abundantly stocked pantry. The
meals were served family-style, in big platters, but in the middle of the
hall was a long buffet table permanently loaded with *zakuski* (appe-

tizers) such as sausage, smoked salmon, and sturgeon, meat and fish in aspic, and sauerkraut. At mealtimes the buffet also held huge tureens of soup, cultured buttermilk, and fruit compote. The lighting was subdued, the appearance somewhat cluttered, and the sanitation may have left something to be desired, but the *kayut kompaniya* certainly had a more homelike atmosphere than the fast-food, cafeteria-style mess decks of American bases.

The class system, which with typical Russian ambiguity is both denied and emphasized, was revealed here with stark clarity; there was a definite hierarchy of officialdom. The *nachalstvo*—expedition leader, deputy leader, base commander, chief engineer—had their own separate table, and their service was a little fancier than the others'. These men enjoyed such refinements as a tablecloth and the traditional Russian tea glasses in metal holders instead of the mugs that the rest of us used. Personnel of intermediate status tended to cluster at the tables surrounding the *nachalstvo's*. For myself, I followed the biblical injunction to take the humblest seat at the banquet—and I stayed there.

In my profession I spend a lot of time working in the field and dining under less than optimum conditions, but to my good fortune I have seldom had many complaints about the food. In the Louisiana bayous, our muddy old quarterboat boasted a Cajun chef who served up platters of ham, chicken, beef, shrimp, and catfish that could have graced the tables of the finest restaurants in New Orleans. At Wilkes Station our Navy cook kept us almost too well fortified with his culinary productions. Mirnyy was no exception, despite the dire reports I had heard about post-Revolutionary Russian cuisine. Nothing was very fancy, but it was good, wholesome food, and there was lots of it.

The basic fare was meat and potatoes, the meat being beef or mutton, though there was some occasional fresh pork from the pigs raised on the base (the idea of livestock farming in the Antarctic always seems to startle Americans as a Soviet vagary, yet Admiral Byrd kept cows at Little America in the 1930s). The meat tended to be tough and stringy, and I could never figure out how they managed to cut it so that a bone always lurked in the middle of each piece, but there was plenty to go around, even after the trimming. On grand occasions the mutton (not lamb, unfortunately) was served as shashlik. Kasha and cabbage were standbys, and sometimes rice or noodles would turn up, but green vegetables were rare. Garlic, pickles, peppers, and the ever-present chopped eggplant overcame the blandness of the diet. We had a plentitude of freshly baked bread, both black and white. I much preferred the dense, tough, slightly sour black variety, which was so tasty that it didn't need anything on it (except, of course, great gobs of butter). But the glory of the meals was the soup. Nowhere else have I savored so many delicious soups: *borshch* (beet), *shchi* (cabbage), *fasol* (bean), fish, rice, potato, and, best of all, black mushroom soup.

Our mealtime beverages were tea, coffee (ready mixed, as at the shelf camp), and, once in a long while, hot chocolate. The tea was served in a highly concentrated form in a special small pot, and one would normally dilute this dense fluid with the desired proportion of boiling water (a ten-to-one ratio was about right for me). Some of the people from Siberia and Central Asia, however, like the aircraft mechanic Fedya, would drink this tannic decoction straight, or mixed with an equal amount of melted butter. Most of the Russians sweetened their tea to what I considered an extraordinary degree, tossing a large number of coarse sugar cubes into each cup or stuffing the sugar into their mouths and drinking the tea through it. It was also customary to flavor the tea with jam, honey, or crushed cranberries.

Breakfast on weekdays was simple: kasha, bread and butter, hard-boiled eggs, and hard, rather greasy sausage. But on Sunday we enjoyed a leisurely brunch that featured *blini* (small pancakes) with sour cream and, to my astonishment, almost unlimited quantities of caviar. For the Russians who didn't like caviar (and they do exist), there was a wide assortment of fruit preserves to garnish their *blini*.

In the evening the *kayut kompaniya* was given over to movies, lectures, chess, dominoes, and discussions. Through the dark, confining winter, Mirnyy engaged in a closely followed radio chess tournament with McMurdo, and the moves in the games were displayed on a large chessboard poster on the wall. As on shipboard, however, the most popular pastime was dominoes. Card games were rare, and there was little overt gambling. Frequent lectures on health and safety under polar conditions, scientific projects of special interest, and current events as related by Radio Moscow could be counted on. Occasionally there would be an open party meeting in which everybody was free to criticize almost everything and everybody on the station. These sessions sometimes became rather heated, especially if some material deficiency or operational fiasco had occurred.

The first major celebration of the year was held in the *kayut kompaniya* on the eve of May Day, shortly after our field party had returned to Mirnyy. It was a gala affair, with the whole base present, and the hall was hung with bright red banners ablaze with political slogans, which, however, were trite, banal, and oddly, even quaintly, dated, as if they had been retrieved from a time capsule of the 1920s (but they were in harmony with the language of Radio Moscow and the posters in our most recent newsreels from Red Square). The multitalented Oskar Krichak was back from his outlying weather stations and had organized an instrumental group that called itself *Sosulka* (Icicle). Oskar had composed a beautiful song, "Svezhii Veter" (Fresh Wind), and it was featured as the musical theme of our expedition, to the spirited orchestration of Sosulka.

We had a long, international musical program. In keeping with the political tone of the event (not that every Soviet holiday doesn't have some political aspect), the German contingent sang a typically Teutonic marching song, "The Workers' Unity Front," which included a lot of militaristic "links, rechts, eins, zwei" in its chorus. When it was my turn I told the crowd, somewhat tongue in cheek, that I would present an old American folk song about a *razboynik* (bandit) who, like the Cossack hero Stenka Razin, "expropriated" the rich and, purportedly, "redistributed" to the poor, and I sang them "The Ballad of Jesse James." Jesse went over very well, so I did an encore of the lugubrious ditty "The Frozen Logger," which fared even better. I gave a brief introduction and résumé of the songs in Russian, sang the lyrics in English, and then my friend Venediktov gave a recapitulation in Russian. The audience admired my dramatic style. Russians tend to be stiff and formal on such public occasions, and there I was, belting out my songs while slouching on the stage with a thumb hooked over my galluses, a genuine *Amerikanetz.*

The spirit of Camp David still glowed over the world political scene, and as the evening wore on there were numerous toasts to *mir i druzhba* (peace and friendship) and to the success of the upcoming Big Four summit conference in Paris, which was to be followed by a visit to the Soviet Union by President Eisenhower. As the toasts progressed I remarked to a friend that it was good that tomorrow was a holiday—there were going to be a lot of nasty headaches around the station. Yes, he joked, if an aggressor ever attacked Russia again, it would probably be on May Day, when everybody in the country has a hangover.

Several days later I was working in the seismological observatory with Boris Kamenetski when he suddenly perked up at something that was coming in from Radio Moscow. "Did you catch that?" he asked.

"I wasn't really listening. It sounded like an American name, Francis Gary Powers, or something. Who might he be?"

"I think we will all know that very soon."

Before long it was announced over the PA system that a very important open party meeting would take place that night. By evening the lurid story about the untimely U-2 flight on the morning of May 1, the downing of the spy plane, and the capture of the pilot, Powers, had come out. I asked Boris, as the ranking Komsomol, if he thought that I, as the only American, should attend the meeting. He replied, "If you are game, we will go together."

It was definitely not a pleasant evening. A lot of the people in the *kayut kompaniya* were clearly surprised that I had had the temerity to show up. Taped speeches by top Soviet leaders, including the initial announcement by Khrushchev, were played, and they were mostly diatribes against the U.S. government. The expedition cadre added their own denunciations, as did several of the rank and file, and the inevitable resolution expressing solidarity with the Fatherland was voted by acclamation. All through this I sat in stony silence with my arms folded and my best poker face on, inwardly reflecting with some bitterness about being betrayed by those unmentionable clowns in Washington, while philosophically recalling the name of the first plane to land at the south pole, *Que será, será* (What will be, will be). Finally, Boris got up and made his statement of the unwavering support of the Mirnyy Komsomol for Soviet policy. But at the conclusion he turned unexpectedly toward me and said, "But let none of this affect our relationship with our good comrade Gil. Whatever problems may exist between our governments, let our personal friendship live on."

His statement received subdued but obviously sincere applause. And although official Soviet-American relations now took a nose-dive into a particularly dark phase, there was no change in the cordial attitude of most of the Russians toward me as an individual. Many of them took a very blasé view of the matter, as when a friend told me, "Not to worry, Gil, it is no big thing. Every taxi driver in Moscow knew about those U-2 flights."

A good deal of concern was directed not only at the international situation, but at the impact on domestic Soviet affairs. Events destroyed the conditions for the "cooperative coexistence" that had appeared to be on the diplomatic horizon. On May 5, the same day that Khrushchev publicly reported the incident, jamming of the Voice of America was resumed after nearly a year of "open airwaves" (this didn't affect our reception in the Antarctic). On May 7, the United States made an admission and justification of espionage, to the bewilderment and consternation of the Russians ("you just don't say things like that"). Although Khrushchev went to the Paris meeting, he stormed out on May 19 after an acrimonious news conference, and despite the pleas of French President Charles de Gaulle and British Prime Minister Harold Macmillan, returned to Moscow. The summit had collapsed, Eisenhower's visit to the U.S.S.R. had been canceled, and the *Kholodnaya Voyna* (Cold War) was back with a vengeance. Now I had a new sense of responsibility. Antarctica seemed to be the only place in the world where Russians and Americans were still on speaking terms.

As to Soviet domestic politics, I heard fear expressed about what this might mean for Khrushchev's leadership, which seemed to be considered the least of several possible evils. Nikita Khrushchev, while apparently at the peak of his power, was far from unchallenged in the Politburo, and such controversial policies as the military cutback early in 1960 had aroused the opposition of strongly entrenched interest groups. The U-2 debacle would surely be used by Khrushchev's enemies and rivals to embarrass him, and while there could always be another summit conference, there might not be another Khrushchev for a long time.

A much more congenial type of flying object for all concerned was orbiting the earth high above us. In April the first meteorological satellite, *Tiros*, had been launched by the United States; little did we know that its infrared pictures of the earth's cloud cover would soon become the staple of television weather broadcasts. Here was a spectacular example of science for peace that cleaned some of the tarnish from our profession's bomb-scarred image. The launching of the first artificial satellite, *Sputnik-1*, on October 4, 1957 (I well remembered our first sighting of it at Wilkes Station), had been the crowning achievement of the IGY, both the symbol of and the impetus for a broadly based popular reawakening of interest in science. Fortunately, triumphs in space had continued at a tempo that reinforced the initial impact: the United States had made its first launch on January 31, 1958, with *Explorer-1*, which promptly made a significant geophysical contribution by revealing the existence of the Van Allen radiation belts of charged atomic particles in the magnetosphere surrounding our planet. In a way, American scientists couldn't help being grateful to the Soviets for launching first, since the catching-up syndrome had elicited enormous financial support from the public purse for our space program, with plenty of spin-off into other fields of research. For the Soviet scientific community there was pride, of course (though they were resigned to being surpassed technologically by the United States as soon as it hit its stride), and something else that reflected the collective memory of the people: a sense of satisfaction that after all that Hitler and Stalin had done to them so recently they could still produce scientific and technological accomplishments that evoked world admiration.

Boris and I continued our routine duties at the observatory, but presently something appeared on our seismograms that was far from routine. On May 22 one of the greatest earthquakes of modern times occurred off the coast of southern Chile. Its magnitude was 8.5 on the Richter scale, it disrupted the earth's surface for hundreds of kilometers along the coast, and it claimed the lives of more than five thousand people. It also created a tsunami, or seismic sea wave, that traversed the Pacific Ocean and reached Japan in twenty-two hours, killing 120 people there. This catastrophe gave strong impetus to the development of the Pacific Sea Wave Warning System in particular, the whole field of geological hazard research and planning in general, and the emerging concept of the complicity of human institutions in "natural" disasters.

Scientifically, the Chilean earthquake had very exciting results: for the first time in history adequate instrumentation was in place to record what are called "free oscillations" of the earth. That is, the huge tremor set the whole earth vibrating as a unit, like a gigantic gong. To carry the musical analogy further, there were many fundamental tones, and each of these had numerous overtones, so the terrestrial "chord" was complex. The frequencies of these vibrations (each wave may last an hour or more) depend on the physical characteristics of the earth, so the disturbances set up by the giant earthquake gave seismologists a means to check and even improve on their previous determinations of the internal structure of the earth—how it is layered with respect to density and elasticity down to, and even inside, its partially molten core.

Little of our time in the *kayut kompaniya* was spent in political rallies. Recreation was paramount, and watching motion pictures was by far the most popular form of entertainment. Mirnyy stocked a large selection of films from many countries. By comparison the cinema library at Wilkes Station (allegedly chosen by a navy chaplain) had been very limited and parochial. Most of the movies were naturally from the Soviet Union and its allies in Eastern Europe, but French, Italian, Indian, Egyptian, Mexican, and Brazilian films were also represented, all with the sound track dubbed into Russian. We also had some American movies and a few from Communist China.

The Chinese films were not exactly smash hits. According to the Russians' snide observations, we had three grades of film—good, bad, and Chinese. They tended to be heavy-handed propaganda pieces with pedestrian plots and stereotyped characters: the stalwart hero who virtuously resisted the evil blandishments of the beautiful female spy and thwarted the machinations of the sinister American officer lurking in the background. What really gave us laughing fits was the way secret messages were invariably passed around on tiny strips of what looked like fortune-cookie paper.

Some of the Czech, Polish, Hungarian, and Yugoslavian movies were excellent, and I was impressed by an East German film that was remarkable in several ways, including the Russians' reaction to it. The setting was Indochina in the 1950s, and the action centered around an airlift operation of the Air America type, manned by a group of uncouth American mercenaries commanded by a tough-

minded, cynical general. The actors who played the flyers were uncannily American in their expressions, actions, and even posture. A
friend asked me if my countrymen would really behave like that—
drinking, brawling, chasing women—and, remembering my recent
stint in the Armed Forces, I replied, "To be honest, yes."

He laughed and said, "Also to be honest, just like us!"

The character of the general who bossed the outfit elicited a certain
grudging appreciation, if not admiration. He was a pragmatic, calcu-
lating man who had no values, perhaps, but knew the exact price of
everything and everybody. The reaction to him ran something like
this: "This is a very sinful person, of course. But in political and business affairs, when you must deal with someone, you want to know
where he stands, and this hard-boiled, matter-of-fact type is infinitely
preferable to the romantic, sentimental idealists."

The plot was fairly simple and was the inverse of a typical American cold war film: the hero, at first another brutal soldier of fortune,
falls in love with a Vietcong spy and is converted to niceness; after
various adventures, they steal a plane and fly off to China in the
sunset. The Russians enjoyed it as fantasy, but were skeptical. They
didn't buy the maudlin Hollywood ending, and they didn't think that
an austere place like Communist China would be much of a place for
a honeymoon.

The Russian movies were often about World War II and its effects
on families, lovers, and friends, and they tended to be long and sad
(not unrealistically). There were a lot of leave-takings, prolonged
separations, and incomplete reunions. Politically oriented movies
frequently focused on a strong, admirable character who unwaver-
ingly forwarded the policies of the regime despite saboteurs, doubt-
ers, and slackers. Films about their revolutionary and civil war period
highlighted the corruption and stupidity of the White generals and
political leaders but, interestingly, did not deny the courage of the
soldiers who fought for them. There were also historical epics about
Alexander Nevsky, Ivan the Terrible, and Peter the Great, lighthearted shows without any great message, and even a couple of zany
musical comedies. A fascinating recurring character in the Russian
films of that era was the good-hearted aunt or grandmother who still
wore a cross at her throat and embarrassed the rest of the family by
asking for a blessing before dinner. The implication was that religion

was all right as long as it was a respectable denomination like Russian Orthodoxy and was taken seriously only by people who were quaint and behind the times. Another stock character was the callow youth who sported loud American-style shirts, loitered on street corners, whistled at girls, and got into trouble with the law.

We had several fine documentary films about science and nature. I remember one superb wildlife movie that would have warmed the heart of Jack Couffer, the freelance photographer who came to Wilkes to obtain footage for Walt Disney. It featured the family lives of polar bears (the Russians call them "white bears"), Siberian tigers, and tundra wolves, and the remarkable Central Asian sport of hunting with the aid of a trained golden eagle. Some of the movie-length cartoons, usually based on Slavic folk tales, were artistically animated. There were many short subjects, including newsreels, reports on economic progress in the Soviet bloc, coverage of sporting events, and "educational films" (very similar to our Army training films), which preached against such evils as alcoholism, factory absenteeism, and religious cults. One extraordinary picture described a new factory in almost religious terms, and I thought, "Only in Russia," but then recalled that it was Calvin Coolidge who had compared a factory to a temple of worship. Among the (unconsciously?) funniest movies I have ever seen was a lyrical short about a modern, mechanized fishing fleet. Impressive shots of giant machines performing various catching and processing operations and glowing descriptions by a narrator with a sonorous, dramatic voice of how efficient, automated, and ultramodern everything was preceded a quick cut to a Chaplinesque little man sitting in the hold surrounded by mountains of fish and cutting their heads and tails off with a paring knife. The Russians cracked up at exactly the same place I did.

When the Soviet traverse party left the south pole, Ed Flowers presented them with a stack of American movie reels. All turned out to be big hits at Mirnyy despite the language barrier. Since my interpreting ability was limited at first, I would briefly paraphrase the dialogue into simple English for the keen-witted Venediktov, and he would translate my version imaginatively to the crowd. We developed into a pretty smooth team. I think the most popular of the American films was a seriocomic Audie Murphy-Dan Duryea western. The Russians could scarcely believe it when I told them that

Audie was one of our most decorated war heroes, but when I did finally convince them it made the second showing a sellout. *The Glenn Miller Story* went over very well, too. Miller and the other big band musicians had many fans in the U.S.S.R., and the fact that he was lost in the war greatly enhanced his stature for our audience. Much of the Russian conception of American cinema and popular music dated from wartime. Several of the older men even wanted to know if we had any Deanna Durbin movies.

The American movies included one real old-timer, *The Man Who Came to Dinner.* Imagine trying to keep up with that rapid-fire Monty Woolley-Jimmy Durante repartee for a foreign audience! *The Joe Louis Story* presented some thorny problems in translating American sports jargon, not to mention the racial overtones. When Joe said, "I've got two strikes against me already," we had to stop the projector for a few minutes of explanation. A movie about a surgeon who after much soul-searching gives up a lucrative high-society prac- tice to serve a mining town brought clucks of approval and nods of recognition: "Just like Russia; all the doctors want to work in Mos- cow or Leningrad and they find ways to avoid the villages." The show-business dialogue in a Phil Silvers musical proved completely intractable, but the spectacular dance routines and the leggy ladies in the chorus saved the show. Some shorts about American football were real crowd-pleasers. The Russians were utterly captivated by the game, and we had to show the scrimmage scenes over and over.

Radio was very big at Mirnyy, too. There were plenty of short- wave receivers around the base, and the personnel were free to listen to anything they chose. Hearing unjammed Voice of America broad- casts was a revelation—and a great disillusionment—for some Rus- sians, who found the forbidden fruit rather tasteless. Maybe jamming was the best thing that ever happened to the turgid and unimaginative VOA of that era. The most respected foreign newscasts were the BBC's. The Russians would sometimes refuse to believe an item I had heard on VOA or U.S. Armed Forces Radio (or something they had heard from Radio Moscow, for that matter), but they would readily accept it when it came from the BBC.

The ubiquitous public address system started its morning program with the Soviet national anthem, the station weather report (and other weather items of note, such as the shockingly low temperature at Vostok), and a tape of the latest news from Radio Moscow. Throughout the rest of the day there were announcements of local interest or importance, introduced by the imperative "*Vnimaniye!*" (attention!), more news and commentary, and tapes of Russian radio shows, entertaining or educational, all interspersed with Russian popular music. A familiar American voice featured regularly on a medley of politically oriented songs: the booming bass of Paul Robeson singing the anthem of the Peoples' Republic of China, "March of the Volunteers," in Chinese. Eventually all my jazz records were taped by the Communications Center, and they became a standard part of the daily program.

Every other Sunday a major social event took place: the *Russkaya banya*, or Russian bath, a traditional cultural institution that combines sanitation with recreation. Ablutions started in an anteroom with a vigorous scrubbing with blistering hot water, strong bar soap, and coarse brushes. Then you entered the steam room and were parboiled for about half an hour in the vapors rising from piles of hot stones beneath the floor slats. If you really wanted to stir the circulatory system you could flagellate yourself with birch branches. Then the hardier souls—and since national honor was somehow at stake, the writer felt obligated to join in—would run outside, regardless of the weather, and dive naked into a snow bank. This was definitely a shock, but it didn't seem to faze some of my companions who belonged to "walrus clubs" and habitually went swimming in Russian rivers at midwinter. Afterwards, we would lounge around the bath house like Roman patricians, drinking ice-cold *kvas* (a fermented fruit drink) or a light wine and reveling in a superb feelng of physical and psychological well-being.

Russians have to be the world's greatest party givers. Any excuse would serve for an evening get-together at Mirnyy. It seemed to be mandatory that everybody have a birthday party, and since there were more than a hundred men at the base a birthday celebration was going on somewhere about once every three days. The major official holidays—May Day, the anniversary of the Bolshevik Revolution, New Year's Day—were occasions for stationwide feasts. But plenty of other things were worth celebrating. Midwinter's Day is traditional for "polar people" of whatever nationality, and the Soviet calendar is full of commemorative days: Army Day, Navy Day, Physical Culture Day, Aviation Day, and so forth. Generally the parties, especially if they were birthdays, involved small groups of friends or administrative sections, but as the American guest I had a standing invitation to practically all of them. If I had liked, my year could have been virtually one long wassail, and I had to be judicious and diplomatic about when to accept and when to decline.

The festive gatherings were invariably high-spirited and good-humored. The strain of ugliness that so often mars American beer brawls at isolated posts seldom crept in. An unpleasant incident arose at one party when a couple of tasteless and somewhat inebriated practical jokers decided to tape-record an uninhibited conversation among their friends secretly. The victims were not at all amused by the playback and demanded immediate destruction of the tape, on pain of dire retribution. Ostensibly they were offended at having their improper language (in which Russian is as abundant as English) recorded for posterity, but I also detected an undertone of outrage at the all-too-familiar implications of electronic eavesdropping. Normally if there were any aggressions to release, dancing was an acceptable physical outlet. Solo dancing in the Russian folk style was often performed during these parties, and sometimes there would be a fierce competition between a couple, or more, of virtuosos. The most extraordinary jumping, kicking, whirling dance I ever saw in my life was performed at a shindig in the *kayut kompaniya* by a fifty-year-old aircraft mechanic.

One party of the many I attended especially sticks in my mind; it was not very long after the U-2 imbroglio, and I found the hospitality that I was shown extremely reassuring. This was near the middle of winter, when the days were getting quite short and violent storms were constantly battering the base. I had received a grandly written formal invitation from a group of workers who lived on the other side of the settlement. The occasion was the birthday of one of their number. A stiff *burya* was blowing, and just getting there would be a problem, but I had worked with these guys and liked them, so I decided to go.

On the way over I had to lean against the pressure of the freezing wind while running up and plunging down the many large snowdrifts that obstructed the path. Squinting through the snow-filled darkness that was broken only by an occasional nebulous guide light, I found the "address" with some difficulty—the building was buried to the roof in snow. I threw open the heavy hatch over the entrance, lowered myself down the access ladder a couple of rungs, and pulled the hatch shut over my head. At the bottom of the entry shaft was a small anteroom, where I shook off the snow and hung up my parka.

At the end of a long, narrow hall was a large room, dimly lit, as usual (do they make anything stronger than a forty-watt bulb in Russia?). They surely do know how to heat a place, though. The building was stifling. The smoky, pungent room was crowded with highly animated people, all seemingly talking and gesturing at once. Most were wearing coarse gray or brown turtleneck sweaters despite the heat, and many were puffing on harsh cigarettes with brand names like "Sputnik," "White Sea," and "Mount Ararat." The range of physical types among the celebrators was enormous: tall, short, fair, ruddy, swarthy, slender, stocky, even a few "typical Russians" (by their own standards) with wide cheekbones and snub noses. (In cartoons and caricatures the Soviet press invariably depicts Americans as tall, lean, angular-featured, and mean-looking. To the disappointment of my hosts, I didn't conform to this image at all, except that early in the morning I'm sort of mean-looking.)

In the center of the room was a long table loaded with the usual delectable *zakuski*: pickles, sauerkraut, sausages, cheese, black bread, and a large, multilayered, heavily frosted birthday cake. Evenly spaced down the middle of the table were several South African soft-drink bottles, which had been refilled with an ominously transparent liquid, the notorious *samogon*. There were also bottles of vodka, cognac, and dark, sweet wines from Armenia and Azerbaijan. I was welcomed with much hugging and backslapping, handed a throat-burning potion and a thick slice of black bread, and invited to join the crowd.

I suppose every country has them. Americans who travel abroad know our own brand all too well, the loudmouthed, blustering, complaining, belittling gringo who makes his countrymen cringe with embarrassment. The Russians also have a characteristic boorish type, the obnoxious national chauvinist, and most of his fellow Russians don't like him any better than anybody else does. One of these bores sidled up to the circle I was in and, out of the blue, began his harange: "In Moscow we have the most beautiful subway in the world!"

Before I could respond, someone else parried, "So who needs a beautiful subway? I don't live in the metro station. I would rather have a beautiful house!"

Another chimed in, "Don't pull that propaganda bunk on our American comrade. He wasn't born yesterday. Here, have a drink and show what you're made of!"

They handed the offender a water glass full of almost pure spirit and kept plying him with it. Someone whispered in my ear, "This provocationist fool is a real pain. We'll put him under the table!" I didn't see the "provocationist" again that evening.

Another kind of unwelcome guest hangs around the fringes of conversations trying not to look too interested but taking mental notes of who said what to whom. This "listener" received the same overwhelming generosity as the "provocationist." And then there was a member of the *nachalstvo* who I'm sure was there only to have a good time, but he, too, was very soon sleeping it off in a corner.

We sat down around the table, cut the cake, and raised toasts, each accompanied by the traditional short speech. When it came my turn, my tongue was already a little thick, but I was told not to worry, as it improved my Russian pronunciation. I toasted the working people of all the nationalities in the Soviet Union, and added a few words of gratuitous advice about hanging together or hanging separately. Here I used a word from an American labor union song which would not acquire quite the same connotation in the Eastern bloc until twenty years later—*solidarnost.*

With the formalities out of the way, the participants sat or stood around eating, drinking, smoking, talking. Somebody put one of my big-band records on an old gramophone. One dancer started a slow, graceful step, another launched into a more lively one. I drifted from one cluster of revelers to another, greeting old buddies, pressing the flesh, adding my two kopecks worth of comment. All kinds of discussions were going on: serious, light, high-minded, and the other kind; you can find as wide a range of opinions on any subject among Russians as among Americans. Of course, most Russian opinions don't appear in the press, but one mustn't assume, as Americans too often do, that just because something doesn't happen in the media, it doesn't happen. For example: "You know," confided a man I was only slightly acquainted with, "when you first came to Mirnyy we thought you were here to spy on us."

I responded, "I can easily understand that."

"The only question was—were you spying for the CIA or the KGB?"

I grinned. "Why not both?" and he went on,

"In these times, nothing is impossible."

"But now people are very open with me, even those I hardly know," I pointed out.

"Now we trust you."

"Why?"

"Instinct, perhaps. The word gets around. You say what you think about your country, about our country, good or bad. Finally, it comes down to this: somewhere, sometime, somehow, you have to trust somebody."

The party broke up around two A.M. and I joined the trickle of guests heading home. The cold air outside delivered a sobering shock to our muzzy heads and flushed faces. The moon had emerged from behind the stormclouds by now, and the wind had subsided, but the ghostly tide of white powder was still running ankle deep, softening the outlines of the rocks, drifts, and buildings, wiping out the footprints of the homeward bound with its currents and eddies.

We had two doctors on the base, a well-equipped dispensary, and a complete operating theater. They were all kept busy treating minor injuries and ailments and a surprising amount of appendicitis. I believe there were seven appendectomies performed at Mirnyy during the year. The physicians also carried out respiratory and circulatory system studies of volunteer subjects, including me. Since I would be living for a prolonged period under severe field conditions if I was chosen to take part in the traverse at the end of the year, they were interested in continuing observations after my return to the United States, and I obtained the cooperation of the Los Angeles Heart Association for that phase of the project.

Another medical research program at Mirnyy, extremely distasteful to many expedition members, was a study of the healing of wounds at low temperatures. The wounds were inflicted surgically on

laboratory dogs that had been brought to the Antarctic for this spe-
cific purpose, but the occasional sight of one of the bandaged canines
never failed to arouse angry complaints against vivisection.

Mirnyy had enough sledge dogs to make up a couple of hauling
teams. These were healthy, lusty creatures that brought back fond
memories of my sledging adventures at Wilkes. The dogs were used
chiefly by Expedition Leader—and Professor—Korotkevich for
journeys along the coast in pursuance of his geographical and biolog-
ical studies. The kennel and the piggery were taken care of by a colorful character everyone called the "pig man," who was the life of any
party with his inexhaustible repertoire of rustic jokes and stories,
mostly off-color, but all hilarious. Several pups were born in the middle of winter, and they all grew rapidly. They were given fanciful
names, like feisty little Mamai (the ferocious Khan of the Golden
Horde of Mongols, who was defeated by the great Russian folk hero
Dmitri Donskoy), Mabus (the name of a cape near Mirnyy; though a
nonsense word to the Russians, this was the surname of an American
airman), Pirat (pirate; he had a black patch around one eye), and the
females Tsygan (Gypsy) and Pulya (bullet). These sledge dogs were
strictly for business, and there was no joy riding or horseplay with
them as there had been with our rather spoiled dog team at Wilkes.
When our airborne geophysical party returned to the ice shelves in
the spring, however, we took little Pulya along as mascot.

The water supply at Antarctic stations is usually a serious problem,
since most of what is available is either too salty or too solid. At
Wilkes we had scooped up snow with a bulldozer and dumped it into
a snow-melter adapted from an old tar-melting machine. At Mirnyy
the procedure was very simple. A huge electrical heating coil was
lowered into the firn a short distance upwind from the base, and the
resulting melt-water pond was pumped out into a tank sledge that
was hauled back to the base by tractor and emptied into a large in-
door tank. The electricity was conducted out by cable from Venediktov's central power plant. This plant was the physical heart of the
whole operation at Mirnyy. Water, heat, light, cooking, communications, machine shop, scientific instruments, all depended on the big,
humming marine diesels in the *Elektrostantsiya*.

Mirnyy, like Wilkes, lies almost exactly on the Antarctic Circle,
and the weather on the Pravda Coast was similar to what I had expe-

rienced three years before. There were the same brief warm spells, even in midwinter, after the sea was blown clear of ice by powerful offshore winds, and the same breathtakingly fine, calm days followed abruptly by storms of terrible violence. Most of the snow that came to us was blown down from the great interior ice sheet by the wind, but occasionally there would be a genuine fall of snow from the clouds. There was something incongruous about those big, soft snowflakes right out of a scene on a Christmas card coming gently down on our stark surroundings. The next wind storm would quickly bare the rocky knobs of this fleecy mantle and heap the snow into massive drifts.

The sea was continually changing. Ice formation on the surface went through stages of congealing, from the delicate *frazil* through the picturesque pancake ice, to its welding into a continuous plate capable of bearing a person, then a vehicle—and then the violent removal of the pack by one of our sudden storms. Vapor rising from the open water often made it look misty, and the mist sometimes thickened into a dense polar fog called *sea smoke*. Occasionally, however, the sea would be glassy and the sky totally cloudless. At those times, with water and sky the same color, the sea horizon would disappear in a "blue-out," and the icebergs and islands that fringe the coast seemed to hover unsupported on the flat azure background.

On June 21, the solar midwinter, the sun barely poked above the horizon just before noon, rested there briefly, then dropped from sight. After that our feeble but cheery friend came back a little more each day, and we had a feeling that we were somehow over the hump, although in fact the bulk of our sojourn still lay before us. The sun was not only something of a personal friend, it provided us with the most spectacular sunrises and sunsets (which at midwinter merged into one) that I have ever witnessed. And shortly after the sun went down the opposite sky would frequently exhibit a diffuse glow or gegenschein of deep purplish hue.

From time to time we would see the extraordinary Novaya Zemlya effect, an optical peculiarity of the polar regions caused by a sharp air temperature inversion. The inversion layer bends the sun's rays upward so that they miss the earth, then reflects them down to strike the earth's surface well over the horizon. The visual result is that after the sun has set it appears to rise again in the same place, finally setting for good when the critical reflecting angle of the rays is reached. There were also frequent colorful spectral phenomena caused by refraction of light through the tiny ice crystals in the cold air. Halos and para-helic circles were commonly observed, and something we would see the sun flanked by brilliant "sun dogs" (parahelia).

The southern lights' auroral zone of maximum frequency centers approximately around the south geomagnetic pole (Vostok Station). It circles to the north of Mirnyy, and hence we were not in the most advantageous location for aurora observations, but we did see many spectacular displays. Beautiful fiery arcs and glowing patches appeared in the night sky, and sometimes bright rays or a curtain of shimmering light converged at the zenith. The colors were usually pastel shades, green or pale white, but occasionally there would be a brilliant red drapery waving and billowing along the northern horizon. The IGY and the launching of *Explorer-1* had been chosen for 1957–58 because those years were at the crest of the eleven-year cycle of solar activity—sunspots, solar flares, and other phenomena—which is closely related across the interplanetary gulf to the aurora and disturbances in the ionosphere (the upper atmospheric layers) and the earth's magnetic field. We were a couple of years past the peak, but the auroral activity was still relatively intense and there were magnetic storms associated with it that interfered with radio communication.

The saddest part of winter was the disappearance of the wildlife population that had made the shore such a lively place in summer and fall. The birds and seals went north to live among the floes as the ice pack spread around the continent. There were no more cackling Adelie penguins, fluttering petrels, or soaring skuas to cheer the sterile landscape. I'm sure that this condition contributed to the prevalent feeling of drawing in on ourselves, an increased awareness of our so vulnerable isolation, a sense of being an outpost not only of man, but of life.

The one striking exception to this northward flight of living creatures was a large emperor penguin breeding area several kilometers across the sea ice from the base. It was an easy distance for a one-day excursion, and visits to this rookery, the intervening icebergs, and nearby Hasswell Islet, which supported a luxuriant growth of lichens and mosses, were a popular outlet for our energy during the confining winter. The emperors, which are between three and four feet tall and weigh seventy or eighty pounds, are several times as big as their more common cousins, the Adelies, and they reverse the usual animal migration pattern. They lay their eggs at coastal rookeries during the winter, and the father penguins incubate them for two freezing months while the mothers fish for food to bring back to the newly hatched chicks. We were careful not to disturb the stately, solemn-looking birds stoically holding their precious eggs off the ice between their webbed feet and downy white belly folds.

The route to the rookery led through a maze of grounded icebergs, not unlike the "iceberg heaven," a place where old icebergs drift off to "die," we had discovered near Wilkes Station. It was an eerie place, heavy with the unique magic of the Antarctic environment. The somber towers evoked images of whited sepulchres. Their distorted shadows stabbed ominously shoreward across the ice. Many of the bergs were hung with huge icicles, which gave them a grizzled, hoary appearance. Here and there a deep crevice revealed the bluish green ice within, betraying its glacial origin. But it was as hard to think of these icebergs as daughters of the land as it is to think of the whale as a descendant of land animals. The ocean with its mystery seemed their native element. It was very still in those floating canyons, for the frozen walls cut off the wind. The sea ice on which we walked seemed solid enough, but surrounding each berg was a forbidding moat of greenish water. After a while the frosted monoliths began to assume dreamlike forms, some enticing, some sinister, all intriguing, and the one just around the next icy corner was always more enchanting than any you had yet seen. It was hard to resist the siren song of this weird realm and the temptation to wander off endlessly among the beckoning icebound hulks.

All this time there was, of course, an abundance of marine life right beneath our feet. It was not ignored by a hardy band of ice fishermen, who could not be discouraged by hours of patient, and numbing, waiting on the wind-swept bay near the station. Their lines dangled optimistically through little holes drilled in the ice. On Midwinter's Day we even held an ice-fishing contest. There were a number of bites, several fish were hooked, a few were landed, and a prize was bestowed for the winning catch, an unappetizing-looking individual of uncertain species that weighed about two kilograms.

The glaciological and geophysical sections, under Ivanov and Senko, respectively, had planned a joint project to keep us occupied during the coldest part of the year: a field investigation of the mass movement of ice and snow from the interior of the continent to the sea in the vicinity of Mirnyy. It had the same general goal and methods as the measurement of glacier movement made by the Wilkes Station glaciologists, whom I had assisted during the IGY. We wanted to draw up a budget for the Antarctic ice sheet: how much water, in the form of snow and hoarfrost, was being accumulated on the continental glacier, as against how much was being removed in the form of ice, snow, and melt-water by various natural processes. The removal, called *ablation*, is caused mainly by the calving of icebergs, but also by snow blowing out to sea during blizzards and run-off of melt-water during the summer. An excess of accumulation over ablation would indicate that the great continental ice sheet is currently being built up, concentrating the earth's surface water in Antarctica and lowering the level of the sea worldwide. An excess of ablation over accumulation would indicate that the ice sheet is wasting away and raising sea level. Our project at Mirnyy was only one of several similar investigations being carried out in those years and continuing into the present. The Antarctic ice is so huge, and its dynamics are so complex that many measurements of different kinds in many places are necessary to get even a rough estimate of what is going on. In 1960 the subject was still of mainly theoretical interest to a small number of specialists. Few even of these could have predicted that the interrelationships of industrial pollution, the composition of the atmosphere, solar energy, climate, the Antarctic ice, and ocean levels would soon become matters of broad public concern.

Our work on the outer glacier slopes in the winter of 1960 was primarily directed at finding the rate at which ice was being carried toward the sea in the sector immediately inland from Mirnyy. To determine this rate we had to know how thick the ice was and how fast it was moving. We could get a fair idea of ice thickness through gravity observations; this was where my gravimeter came in handy. Measurement of the ice flow required the precise geodetic location of movement stakes at regular intervals, and the frequent replacement of the stakes as they blew down, broke off, dropped into crevasses, and so on. Our fixed control base, for both the gravimetric and geodetic surveys, was the granitic-gneissic outcrop called Komsomolskaya Hill, which rises to a crest of 35 meters (115 feet) between Mirnyy Station and the shore.

Over a period of several months we managed to establish a grid of data points on the glacier within commuting distance of Mirnyy; we called it the Glaciological Polygon. Our work in this region was a bit hazardous, since the ice surface was badly crevassed and a violent *purga* (blizzard) was liable to come howling down from the interior plateau at any moment. In midwinter we had gale-force winds every other day, on the average, and in September, every single day. The temperature dropped to around thirty below, and the fine snow particles that were almost constantly suspended in the air intensified the chilling effect of the wind. No matter how warmly you were dressed, that cruel blast got through to you after a couple of hours, and when it did you could stamp and jump and shake all you wanted, but there was really nothing to do but suffer. The wind, the slippery ice, and the extremely broken surface required that we use mountain-climbing procedures, roping up, wielding ice axes, and wearing crampons on our boots.

Vyacheslav Ivanov was in charge of the field operations; his extensive mountaineering experience in the Caucasus and Pamir mountains (the Pamir, in Central Asia, are of near-Himalayan height) was put to good effect in training and preparing us for iceclimbing and glacier travel and in leading us through the crevasse fields and icefalls. Sometimes he seemed like a grouchy and pedantic perfectionist, but that was because he was fanatically conscientious about the safety of our group—more than one of his climbing companions had perished in the mountains. Normally we worked in two fifty-meter ropes of three men each, with Ivanov leading the first rope and our drilling engineer, Boris Zakhariev, leading the second. Boris was also a skilled alpinist. He was stocky, imperturbable, and very tough, and he had an amazing immunity to the cold.

Vitaly Tsukernik, Petr Bezukladnikov, and I were joined by a young physicist, Pavel Kutuzov, to make up the rest of the party. Pavel and I hit it off right away when I remarked that he had the surname of the Russian general who had led the army opposing Napoleon in 1812. He was a good-natured, idealistic fellow, one of the new generation of intellectual Komsomols, who enjoyed arguing with me about politics and could do so without rancor, in a mutual spirit of friendly persuasion. I was already fully familiar with Vitaly's energy, intensity, and dedication in the field, and with Petr's easy-going, folksy demeanor, which concealed an astonishing breadth of both scientific and worldly knowledge. He didn't talk a lot, but he had a dry sense of humor that occasionally surfaced in a terse comment.

The lobe of the ice sheet flowing down to the sea at Mirnyy is obstructed by bedrock mountains, most of which are covered by the ice, but a few barely jut above the glacier surface as *nunataks*. The obstruction they cause to the ice flow causes widespread fracturing inland from the station. There is a tortuous but safe route through the crevasses that is used for vehicle traffic to the interior. We would ride up this well-marked trail to the polygon in one of the personnel carriers, which we might then use to get around parts of the survey area if motorized travel seemed safe.

The trip was often fascinating. Optical effects on the inland ice, where there are frequent temperature inversions, can be startling. Sometimes when you are driving along you get the impression that you are entering a valley. The sides seem to become steeper and steeper, but you know very well from previous trips that the slopes are not increasing at this location. You make a ninety-degree turn, and the "valley" follows you right around; you drive another kilometer and look back—and it has completely disappeared. A distant building appears before you as a small dot, suddenly seems very large and close, then abruptly vanishes. It reappears upside down, loses its doors and windows, regains them, then assumes various outlandish shapes. The moon looks like a golden mushroom, a celestial football, or a long-necked gourd. Mirage lakes appear along the inland horizon, while out to sea the icebergs and islands loom far above the horizon and appear to be inverted.

At times we encountered whiteout conditions. A true whiteout—not to be confused with a blizzard—occurs when a low-lying cloud layer allows some sunlight to pass through it, and the light is then almost totally reflected from the snow surface below. Much of it is re-reflected by the underside of the cloud layer, and so on, to produce a luminous greenhouse effect: with light being reflected from all directions, shadow is eliminated, surface relief cannot be discerned, and the distinction between snow and sky disappears. There is no visual horizon. In an extreme whiteout you seem to be floating in a homogeneous white haze, a condition that is apt to induce vertigo. This is obviously dangerous for a pilot trying to land an airplane, and a tractor driver can easily lose his bearings until he drives in circles and cannot make out if there is a hill or a gully in front of him. These conditions became more common as the sun climbed higher in the sky after midwinter.

Just as the Antarctic continental glacier is gigantic, so the features of the glacier surface are on a giant scale. The crevasses are stupendous chasms in which you could easily lose a house or a whole rope of climbers. In winter most of them were spanned by snow bridges, some solid enough to drive a tank over, others dangerously fragile and requiring a lot of probing with the point of ice axe to determine if they were passable. Sometimes the crevasses were completely bridged over, but usually there was enough of a depression to guess where they were, unless a whiteout obscured any traces. The roped parties moved in a tentative, gingerly manner—from the air they must have looked like a couple of caterpillars—treating the glacier with due respect. While the lead man probed for a crossing, the number two man belayed him. If the first man fell, the second was to hold the belay while the third came around, probing all the while for other crevasses, and tried to help the fallen leader. If the other rope of climbers was in the vicinity, they would come to the rescue, too. My companions appreciated the saying I had learned from the Wilkes glaciologists: if you fall into a crevasse, there's one consolation—in a hundred years you'll be in better shape than the guy who didn't.

We had a few close calls on the ice. Once when I was on Boris's rope, with Petr at the tail end hand-carrying his heavy, bulky Soviet model gravimeter, we entered a region of chaotic grandeur, an awesome scene of frozen violence. The crevasses were arranged in a crazy pattern of both challenge and camouflage: some were glaringly, shockingly exposed, down to their aquamarine, seemingly bottomless depths, while others were lying like booby traps beneath deceptive swirls of snow that resembled meringue or cotton candy. A low partial cloud cover softened the shadows, and a gusty breeze nipped at our faces.

While crossing a flat expanse of wind-hardened snow I suddenly felt a tug at the rope that was coiled around my waist and harnessed to my shoulders, and I glanced back toward Petr. Petr had vanished. I yelled "*Spasitye!*" (Help!) to Boris, reversed direction, and dug down with my ice axe in an instinctive self-arrest. While I belayed the tautening line, Boris circled around like a big cat, lowered himself to a prone position, and cautiously peered into a small round hole in the snow. Just below the aperture Petr was now dangling over a cavernous crevasse, still clutching the handle of his gravimeter. Boris and I had both crossed an apparently secure snow bridge when it inexplicably gave way under Petr alone, and he found himself hanging, by the best of fortune, upright, with his head a couple of feet below the top of the hole and his boots a couple of hundred feet above the bottom of the crevasse.

After Boris and I had laboriously hauled him out—happily, he was uninjured and able to help himself to some extent—I told him that his retention of the heavy scientific instrument under these circumstances was above and beyond the call of duty. Petr replied in this vein: "If you only knew the amount of paperwork I would have had to fill out if I had lost it, you wouldn't be surprised."

"Ah, yes," I acknowledged, "I've worked for the government, too."

My companions gave me more credit than I deserved for this episode; it was largely a matter of drill, thanks to Ivanov and Zakhariev. On the ice you don't trifle with "acceptable risk" in technique or technology: there are quite enough risks waiting for you out there in nature. And when you are three on a rope, with each climber's life dependent upon his fellows, you don't have to read a treatise about the brotherhood of man. You are living it.

My room, despite how small it was, became a center of attraction as the winter wore on. People squeezed in to hear my jazz records and lined up to borrow them for parties or for taping. The Dixieland and big-band pieces were more popular for the party trade than the relatively esoteric modern jazz, which was, however, of great interest to our resident orchestra leader and composer, Oskar Krichak. Imagine my surprise when at one banquet I heard the unmistakable voices of Elvis Presley and Pat Boone, who were not in my collection. It turned out that these records had been brought down by a young man who had obtained them while serving on a technical-assistance mission to Egypt. I'm not suggesting that the United States' loss of the Aswan Dam project to the Soviets resulted in the introduction of rock and roll into Russia, but still, the world often works in stranger ways than are dreamed of by the people who sit up late at night in chancelleries.

Russian custom says that if someone admires a possession of yours, you should offer it to him, while you may expect to receive something of his in return. Thus it was that the original objects in my room were steadily being replaced by substitutes of more or less usefulness. Eventually, even the substitutes were being replaced. I also handed out my ample stock of office and medical supplies freely. Among the most treasured of these were such commonplace products as Band-aids, paper clips, cellophane tape, and ballpoint pens. I'll never forget the ingenuous delight of a man who came in with a cut finger when I casually wrapped a plastic bandage around it. Such minor medical conveniences were virtually unknown in the Soviet Union. I built up a pretty good cut-and-bruise practice, and Dr. Shastin, the younger and more amiable of our two physicians, jovially suggested that I hang out a shingle.

Most of the books in my cultural-exchange collection were eventually donated to the base library, though a number of them went to friends who showed special interest in a particular volume. Fedyukhin, the photographer and war veteran, keenly appreciated Bill Mauldin's World War II cartoons, so I gave him my personal copy of *Up Front*; in return I received a Soviet-made exposure meter.

There was no shortage of ordinary lead pencils at the base. They were all inscribed "Sakko i Vanzetti" (Sacco and Vanzetti) for the name of the factory in which they were manufactured. I wondered how many of the millions of government bureaucrats pushing these pencils throughout the length and breadth of the Soviet Union were aware that the two Italian immigrants so honored had been anarchists dedicated to abolishing the political state completely.

I had not taken any food with me from the United States, and if I wanted an afternoon or evening snack in Building Five the makings were quite limited—usually hardtack biscuits with jam, honey, or chopped eggplant, and a salami-type sausage. Hardtack, I was told, had been one of Stalin's fixed ideas ("iron rations" for the masses) and even seven years after his passing, quantities of the unsalable stuff were still being unloaded on recipients unlikely to look a gift horse in the mouth—like expeditions. Somehow this reminded me of the World War II C-rations the U.S. Army had been feeding my outfit in 1954. Early on, I began to wish that I had at least brought some peanut butter, and after a while I started to have cravings for hot dogs and dreams about hamburgers with the works.

The German scientists had shown more foresight in the matter of ethnic food. When I visited them in the isolated under-snow bunker where they were quartered I would be treated to German sausage, cheese, and bread, and a little schnapps—plus a great deal of warm hospitality. They did not always receive the same from the Russians, for they had a considerable hurdle of national resentment to overcome: that they were Germans from a democratic republic that espoused socialism didn't cut any ice with those who still nursed a lot of bitterness from the war.

Skeib had an excellent command of English, but when we were in company we would always courteously speak Russian in our contrasting accents, to the amusement of the Russian listeners. Sometimes in the *kayut kompaniya* the Germans would huddle at a table and converse in their own language while everyone else in the room was speaking Russian; the vocal effect was extraordinary, as the chopped, guttural regularity of German was superimposed on the turbulent river of words that is Russian.

A couple of nights each week I assisted in an English-language class that had been organized by our versatile engineer, Venediktov. The students were eager to hear a native speaker, though I warned them that my pronunciation had been influenced by living in regions of strong dialect, like marvelously polyglot Brooklyn, the southern Appalachians, and Pennsylvania Dutch country. They conceded that I spoke Russian with an odd accent, that I almost sounded like a Gruzinski (Georgian). They claimed that when I pronounced the word *uzhas* (awful—a very common word in Russian) it sounded just the way that late son of Georgia, Josef Stalin, had said it.

The language circle usually consisted of about a dozen men. The Russians had their own textbook of English grammar and some lesson books, and I provided a Russian-English dictionary. My main contribution was to assist with pronunciation and colloquialisms, but I also gave little lectures on American geography and history, illustrated with my own slides, and a history of jazz and popular music, with the help of my records. The students were required to read original compositions, which were subject to my grammatical corrections. These stories often told about adventures on a *komandirovka*, a special assignment that could involve a trip to a distant part of the Soviet Union, and I obtained a pretty good education from them myself.

Russians are great lovers of puns. After we had discussed words like success, access, excess, and so forth, one student read a long story about his visit to Leningrad when he was a sailor in the Baltic fleet. It seems that he met a girl, as sailors are wont to do, and they visited the usual tourist spots—the Winter Palace, the Alexander Column, the Bronze Horseman. At the conclusion they were kissing goodbye on the Nevsky Prospekt. After a brief pause, one of the group asked impatiently, "Well, what about it, were you suc-sexful?"

A frequent onlooker but not a participant at the classes was the base commander. He was a hard-liner with a limited English vocabulary, and he used to greet me with memorized pleasantries like, "Good morning. There are many fascists in America, yes? Goodbye."

I tended to respond in kind, and our relationship was not terribly cordial. Apparently he didn't like some of the things he heard at the class, either, and more than once I indirectly received a few words to the wise about the content of my lectures.

Despite this unpromising beginning, the commander seemed to take a liking to me after a while, and even started inviting me to his room in the Pentagon for tea. This became a subject of amusement among the other Russians. What on earth did we have to talk about? It turned out that he was actually very curious about America, especially California, and most of all San Francisco, the city of which Chairman Khrushchev had spoken so well. With this kind of encouragement I opened up like a real chamber-of-commerce booster, going so far as to draw him a map showing such strategic locations as the Cow Palace, Fisherman's Wharf, the Tenderloin, North Beach, and Chinatown.

I had started growing a beard upon arrival in Mirnyy, but soon became aware that I was alone in this respect. Beards, it seemed, were definitely out in the Soviet Union in those days, despite the popularity of Fidel Castro, who had come to power the previous year, and I found myself looked upon with disapproval by the arbiters of public taste; the base commander referred to me derisively as the "bishop" or the "rabbi." I persevered, however, and before long I was joined by a few other nonshavers here and there. Then the thing began to snowball, and soon whiskers were sprouting from chins all over the station. Eventually, when it was realized, I suppose, that there was nothing all that subversive about hair on the face, beards became in at Mirnyy and, mirabile dictu, we even had a contest for the best beard in the settlement. My shaggy, ginger-colored growth took first prize, but I suspect that this was not so much for aesthetic reasons as for having given encouragement to the other bearded ones.

Controversy over beards in the polar regions was actually nothing new. There have long been those who say that the beard protects the face from cold, that shaving removes protective oils, and that, in effect, the good Lord (or nature, if you prefer) put beards there for a purpose, so why not use them? The anti-beard faction says that beards may prevent the detection of frostbite and that their insulating effect is nullified by the accumulation of hoarfrost, that is, that the beard was not designed for such a cold climate. But then there are the claims of tradition, and in the slovenly, profane, bearish atmosphere of a polar station it just seems out of place to have people carefully grooming their faces every morning. I have always grown a beard in the field, but it is primarily from laziness. I would not deny that a beard can be inconvenient. Once I came in from the cold with my whiskers so securely frozen to my balaclava headgear that I had to thaw the whole mess out for about five minutes before I could drink a cup of coffee.

By midwinter drifted snow filled in all the space between the buildings, and in most cases the only access was through the trapdoor in the roof. It was funny to poke your head out in the morning and see all around you other heads sticking up out of their trapdoors like so many gophers or prairie dogs. There was one prominent feature that still broke through the surface of the snow in the middle of the base, a steam pipe with a large expansion loop in the shape of a question mark. One morning I pointed to it and jested to my friend Petr, who was emerging from the roof of an adjacent building, "Is that the symbol of our expedition?"

He replied, "Not only of our expedition, comrade, but of our time!"

The "International Brigade" offloading supplies from the *Kooperatsiya*.

Zavadovski Camp on the West Ice Shelf.

The Transport Section with some of its rolling stock. Section Leader Krasnikov second from left.

Emperor penguins on the march.

Edge of the continent: coastal ice cliffs, with sea ice in the foreground. Note tent at base of cliff.

Mirnyy Station, with *nunatak* in foreground .

Sosulka in action. Kamenetsky on drums, Krichak at pinao.

Fedya Kovalenko pours a beer for the author in the mess hall.

The *Nachalstvo*: (from left) Matveychuk (deputy leader), Korotkevich (leader), Maltsev (navigator), Golubenkov (base commander).

Drilling a seismic shot-hole on the West Ice Shelf.

Circling the wagons: Using the log in chain-hoisting the diesel engines for repair.

Airdrop of fuel drum (bottom left) by LI-2 at Komsomolskaya.

6

Conversations with the Comrades

It ain't so much what we don't know; it's that we
know so much that ain't so.

—*Josh Billings*

The Russians are great, one might almost say obsessive, conversationalists, and a place like Mirnyy, especially in the rather slow-paced winter, offers splendid opportunities to hold lengthy confabulations. Most of my companions seemed to want the *Americanetz* to hear what they had to say, and I became party to innumerable discussions on an unlimited variety of topics. At first I could join in the bull sessions only with difficulty, and I kept a little notebook with me at all times to jot down unfamiliar words or expressions so I could ask about them or look them up later in my dictionary. My friends were sympathetic: "We know Russian must be a hard language for you; we have trouble with it ourselves!" Sometimes, as when the pig man was telling one of his bawdy tales, they would laugh at my quizzical expression: "You won't find *that* word in your dictionary!"

However, as I became more adept with their language, especially in the latter part of the year, when I was thinking "po-russki" (in Russian), I found that it is a marvelous vehicle of communication. By that

101

time, the strangeness that most Americans usually attribute to the Slavic peoples had dissipated, and I felt entirely at home with my hosts.

The experience of the small number of Americans who have served with Soviet expeditions is unique. A visit to an isolated foreign station is in some ways like a visit to the mother country. Indeed, it concentrates the essence of that nation much the way an ancient ship concentrates for archeologists the artifacts of a lost culture. In the case of a closed society like the U.S.S.R., it may be even more revealing. No traveler in the Soviet Union, no matter how good his command of the language, no diplomat or journalist, no matter how long he has lived there, can fully break down the official barriers and establish the personal rapport that comes with living and working cheek-by-jowl with a group of people under conditions of uninhibited fellowship. One might go so far as to say that nobody who has not passed the bottle with the Russians can speak with any authority of their country. Furthermore, expedition people come from many walks of life—scientists from the academy, engineers from industry, aircraft pilots and navigators and mechanics from the services, specialized craftsmen and manual laborers from various backgrounds, Party activists and administrative functionaries from rigorous training programs. In general they have seen a good deal more of their homeland than most of their fellow citizens, and they represent a wide range of ages and ethnic groups (though only one sex). For this reason, I feel a certain obligation to recount some of the things I learned from talking with these fascinating people about themselves and their zealously guarded society while living in this little Russia in the Antarctic. I also feel a sense of duty to give voice to the seldom-heard working people of the Soviet Union, whose real history is yet to be written.

First of all, let me remark that I was more often struck by the similarities between Russians and Americans than by the differences. This may be partly because at the start I expected to find much greater contrasts. But perhaps it also helps to have a quasi-Southern heritage and the particular, and often ambivalent, outlook that comes with it. There are many profound differences in the two societies, of course, but I discovered that they are sometimes the opposite of what one would believe from the verbal smokescreens that the Cold

War propagandists on both sides have blown out. Simplistic, stereo-typed views are peculiarly misleading in dealing with things Russian, for in that country above all there is a chasm between theory and practice, formality and reality. George Orwell is thus an invaluable traveling companion, and the "Potemkin Village" a chastening concept. The Russians may not have invented the kind of semantic subterfuge that Orwell dissected, but they must hold quite a few patents in the field.

By now, it should not surprise anyone to hear that the Soviet Union, like the United States, is a fiercely competitive, money-oriented, corporate society, and that it has all the social ills that follow therefrom. I would guess that individual competition in some spheres is more intense in Russia, particularly in the pursuit of quality higher education and rewarding jobs in science and technology. But that's not all. There is an extraordinarily intricate system of monetary and other incentives specifically designed to arouse competitive spirit. It goes far beyond anything else I have encountered in my career in university, government, and industrial research. The reality of the Soviet economy is a species of Social Darwinism that is the complete antithesis of the ritualistic, mummified official ideology, which for all its relevance might as well be chanted in Old Church Slavonic.

The basic incentive system for workers in the remoter and more inclement parts of Soviet Russia was set up in 1932, at the height of Stalin's campaign against the sin of "egalitarianism." In general, it promised special advantages in annual leave, pension rights, educational opportunities, and housing, plus an adjustment in base pay, the *severnaya nadlavka* (northern increment). Later decrees altered the incentives and the areas considered those of extreme hardship, but essentially the wage plan called for an increase in base pay of ten percent every year or six months, depending on the severity of the working conditions, up to a maximum of eighty percent (as of February, 1960), and it applied to the Soviet Arctic and eastern Siberia.

In *Antarktida* there was a similar system, with additional bonuses. For example, a junior scientific observer might make about 1200 (old) rubles per month in Moscow (there was a currency adjustment in 1961 of ten to one, so this wage became 120 new rubles; it was worth about $130 at the official exchange rate). If this was his first year in the polar regions, the *polyarnik* would receive only the minimum increment, but he would also get 250 rubles per diem for "special hardship." Thus he would earn approximately a nominal $6,000 (in 1960 dollars) for the year, a very substantial income for a Soviet citizen. For many of the personnel their Antarctic salaries gave them the means to make a major purchase that would otherwise be out of reach, like an automobile or a small *dacha* (vacation cottage). In fact, several slots at the head of the waiting list for cars were reserved for expedition members, a valuable privilege by itself when people were waiting years for a new car. Of course, the base pay for an American worker in the Antarctic Program was much higher, but the Soviet increment to provide extra incentive—about 300 percent—was proportionately much greater than my Antarctic hardship bonus of 40 percent.

Food and lodging at the base were gratis, of course, but nevertheless, careful accounts were kept (there was an accountant attached to the expedition, and at one of the general meetings someone indignantly deplored the presence of a "paper-shuffler" when we needed more "producers"; actually, he was a very decent chap). The food allowance was pegged at 900 (old) rubles per man per month. This represented a lot of chow, even at a camp where much hard physical labor was done in the cold outdoors, and usually it was not all consumed. We received the uneaten balance in candy, rather than cash: much of the confectionery ration, especially the chocolate, which is a rare delicacy in Russia, was saved up for children back home or for trading purposes.

At Wilkes Station, my work with explosives had earned special demolition pay for the Seabees involved. Similarly, at Mirnyy, certain categories of workers could qualify for special incentives. Flight crews and airborne work parties like our geophysical-glaciological group received a hazardous duty allowance for every touchdown and takeoff in the field, and the men at Vostok received extra compensation for the severe conditions at their isolated station. In these cases, the bonuses amounted to substantial percentages, even multiples, of the base pay. They also had the interesting side-effect of encouraging many short trips rather than a few long ones.

Overall, I found the Russian attitude toward money and what it can buy to be very similar to my own countrymen's. I suspect that the Soviet economic man is very much like the American, minus the car and mortgage. There is certainly the same intense desire for consumer goods. There does not, however, seem to be the same admiration for the conspicuous consumer. I found the Russians to be as much individualists and hedonists as Americans, but at the same time the images of asceticism and collectivism appealed to them. Dostoyevski said it all: the interplay of self-indulgence and self-flagellation is a recurring theme in the Russian character and in Russian history.

The Russian *polyarniki* were generally older men, well established in their careers, and they were perhaps more motivated by practical considerations than the typically more youthful and footloose Americans working in the Antarctic. Nevertheless, they were as much intrigued by the tradition and mystique of polar exploration as my American colleagues had been during the IGY. They spoke reverently of Scott, Amundsen, and Byrd, and the word *geroi* (hero), which is frequently used sarcastically in the Soviet Union because it has been squandered so much on political hacks, was bestowed on the early Antarctic discoverers with obvious sincerity. But I found that the greatest polar hero in the Russian pantheon was, not surprisingly, the Norwegian scientist, Arctic explorer, and humanitarian Fridtjof Nansen, whose mission to Russia after World War I to direct famine relief and the exchange of prisoners of war is still remembered with gratitude.

Science was our reason for being in the Antarctic, so we often had occasion to compare notes on the scientific establishments of our countries. When talk got around to the funding of research projects, I learned that a familiar rationale was very much in style in both nations as a means of extracting money from government pursestring holders. When asked how grants were obtained for research in America, I explained (with tongue only partly in cheek): "Well, first the scientist describes the catastrophic consequences if this particular line of inquiry is not pursued (this ploy is called *catastrophism*). If that doesn't work, he then points out that the Russians have a similar project of unknown but probably menacing magnitude under way, and they are going to beat us to it, whatever it is, if we don't start moving. This is the clincher—the mere fact that the Russians are doing it ensures that it is vitally important, because everybody knows that you are ten feet tall."

My friends laughed uproariously. "Just like us, only we use the American threat, of course."

I learned that the Soviet scientific community, like our own, goes in for crash programs in a big way. Khrushchev was noted for pushing pet projects without any regard for the dislocations they might bring in the rest of the system (the characteristic Russian failing of not seeing the whole for the parts). Crash programs' repute can be gauged by the hearty "amens" I received when I repeated a bon mot cribbed from a lecture by nuclear physicist Victor Weisskopf, namely, "A crash program is like trying to get a baby in one month by making nine women pregnant."

I got a lot of mileage out of pulling the Khrushchevian trick of expounding old American sayings that were usually thought up on the spur of the moment. The Russians responded in kind, and the amount of instant folk wisdom that was purveyed at Mirnyy during my stay was astonishing.

As the example above suggests, the problems that scientists and engineers face in the two societies are often strikingly similar. Significant differences, however, also exist. One of our discussions on this subject went pretty much as follows, with me saying, "What would you say are the biggest difficulties in your work in the Soviet Union?"

"Careerism is the real bane of our profession and of our whole society. The almighty career is fatherland, ideology, religion, and family for far too many of us," might be the reply, to which another Russian would add,

"Yes, an awful lot of intellectual energy is wasted in scrambling up the promotion ladder, maneuvering for advantageous positions, building reputations, forming cliques of patrons and protégés who scratch each other's backs. There is too much laboratory politics, undercutting your rivals, backbiting. It's a matter of competition for too few good jobs."

I responded, "Sounds familiar. How about the relations between organizations?"

My friend did not mince words: "They are generally destructive: pirating of personnel and equipment, attacks on each other's work, petty jealousy, and feuding. They're all squabbling over funds. And we're too close together for comfort. Too many of the institutes are clustered in Moscow and Leningrad. Did you notice how many of us are from those two cities?"

As a point of curiosity, I would ask, "What about political interference? In one state where I lived the library system was headed by a virtual illiterate who had been appointed because he was a loyal political hack. Do you have that sort of thing?"

"Oh yes—Lysenko is still around! But there is not so much as in Stalin's day, thank God. Now when we get incompetents in charge it is usually a matter of seniority, personal influence, sometimes nepotism. There's still a cult of the individual leader—they all want to be autocrats, especially the hidebound, narrow-minded old fogies who head departments for too long and keep the young people down and new ideas out. Our institutions are very conservative."

A colleague of his expanded somewhat as follows: "Another thing inherited from the Stalinist era has a real stranglehold on innovation—the fetish of security. It's a Pavlovian reflex. No one wants to tell anyone else anything. The first response to a question is always, 'Why do you want to know that?' Science suffers from these absurdly defensive attitudes, but they have an inertia of their own. We have better access to the world literature in our scientific fields than to what our colleagues in our own country are doing."

A further Russian complaint could be, "Another problem is false economy. It's a throwback to the days of scarcity, and we haven't gotten over it yet. There wouldn't be so many shortages if there wasn't so much hoarding, but there is no sense of sharing at all. And there's so much nitpicking over every little expense that the overall goal is lost sight of."

"We have an expression in America, 'publish or perish.' Do you think there's overemphasis on being published in journals in your country?"

"Definitely! And it's based on sheer quantity, not quality. You get a promotion by the gross weight of your papers, not their content."

Here a kibitzer would join in. "Yes, you theoretical scientists love to turn out endless publications that are of no use to us engineers whatsoever! There's far too little contact between pure science and technological applications."

"Indeed! And what kind of support do we get from the technical industries? Some of the experimental equipment they send us is scandalous!"

I would try to head off a shouting match. "So there's a gap between research and development?"

"A gap—there's a canyon. In Russia it's more like 'research versus development.' Basic research, design, production, quality control, distribution—all are separate worlds, and there is very little feedback."

Enter a Russian apologist: "Well, I don't mean to just make excuses, but after all, Russia is only a generation away from a peasant economy, and not very far removed from serfdom. In the last half-century we have had two world wars, a revolution, and a civil war, all fought on our own territory. Everything that had been built up was repeatedly destroyed. You told us in class, Gil, about your own civil war, the last war fought on your soil. How long did it take your Southern states to recover?"

"Ah, you were taking notes! Well, it took several generations; in some places the effects are still felt—and some people I know think they are still fighting it."

Since both of my expedition sections spent a lot of time dealing with logistical problems, I became pretty familiar with the production and procurement setup in the Soviet Union. Fortunately, I was able to hear a spectrum of viewpoints: from people who had been in the managerial chain of command, the technical staff, and the assembly-line workforce of Soviet industry. I have drawn a few generalizations from these impressions, projected as they are through the interpretive lens of a midtwentieth century American technologist.

Russian society contains an odd mixture of feudal, capitalist, and bureaucratic-statist elements. One thing it totally lacks is any sort of control by workers' councils (soviets). I call it "feudal" because the economic structure (military and civil—there is little difference) is compartmentalized into innumerable cellular fiefdoms, each more or less self-sufficient and in continual conflict with its neighbors; and because power is commonly exerted through hierarchies based on personal loyalty, patronage, and family ties. The roots of this system (perhaps) go back to the manorial estates of the nobles and the subsistence economies of the ancient peasant communes. If so, the system has surely been reinforced by the scarcity and uncertainty that have prevailed in modern times, which for Russians have truly been dark ages. Nobody can say, "We planned it that way." The model for the Soviet economy is Topsy. Such a system was, however, quite acceptable to Stalin, that militant cynic most responsible for its present form, for it fitted well with his principle of divide and rule. It is a great mistake to suppose that a dictator wants a monolithic society under him. That would be far too dangerous, since it might turn solidly against him. The successful tyrant exploits the divisions in society and even creates them where they don't already exist.

The popular image of the totalitarian state is much too simplified really to fit the Russian case. If Soviet Russia is looked on as some kind of huge drill team, it is one in which at the command "right face" some members turn right while dragging their heels, some turn left, some do an about face, and the rest (most, perhaps) just loiter around drinking, smoking, and griping.

Part of this medieval aspect of Russian society involves the lack of those unifying principles and institutions that are taken for granted in modern Western societies, like the King's Highway, or its modern derivative, the interstate freeway system. With us, the concept that goods and people should travel freely without every little barony along the route making its own exactions has long been accepted unquestioningly (at least within our national borders), and the occasional tollgate is viewed as an irritating anachronism. But in the Soviet Union, on the contrary, it is fatalistically understood that local authorities will arbitrarily toll, tax, impede, impound, or confiscate anything that comes down the pike. The trains not only fail to run on time, they may disappear—seemingly from the face of the earth—between one station and the next. This universal practice of short-stopping throughout the transportation network inevitably reinforces the existing tendencies toward hoarding and autarchy in each little fiefdom.

A characteristically Russian form of hoarding is referred to sardonically as "industrial virginity." Any machine or fixture or piece of material that is in pristine condition is considered far too valuable to be subjected to the bruising productive process, but equipment that is flawed or old and broken down is used long past its economic life and repaired, more or less, far beyond the point of diminishing returns. The immaculate items eventually become old maids, obsolete before they are ever used. In the United States we feel, "If it works, don't fix it." The Russian version is more likely to be: "If it works, don't use it."

The feudal analogy is not my invention. When I asked a skilled craftsman, who had learned his trade in the army but had grown up as a peasant, about collective farming, he responded heatedly, "And just what is a 'collective farm'? A monastery vineyard is a kind of collective farm. So is a colonial plantation or an estate worked by serfs. Stalin just brought back serfdom, with himself as the feudal lord, and called it 'collective.' "

A great deal has been written about central planning in the Soviet Union: it is too bad to have to report that it is another Potemkin Village. (It was also illuminating to learn that, so very typically, the Soviet planning effort from its inception was not based on the theories of Karl Marx, but was pragmatically copied from the military mobilization program of imperial Germany in World War I!). There is a plan for the economy, of course (Khrushchev's Seven-Year Plan was promulgated with much fanfare in 1959), but it merely reflects the current front lines of the perpetual power struggle over which industrial warlord gets how much investment capital. Its projections are subject to change without notice, its statistics are based on disinformation (does the lackey tell his lord how bad things are?) and its concrete effect is practically nil. In short, "The Plan" is a big joke in the Soviet Union: it seems to be taken seriously only in the West. I came to realize that only people who are used to the relative order and discipline of more stable societies could possibly imagine a "planned economy" in Russia. The turbulence, the lack of integration, the dissonance—the background noise and defective feedback, to put it in technological language—result in a qualitative difference that must be lived to be appreciated. One could add that it is axiomatic that there can be no effective planning in a complex society without freedom of information, and this alone disqualifies the U.S.S.R. from the word go. It may be a "command economy," but it is not an "obey economy."

While the "visible hand" of state control is largely an empty glove, I heard plenty about Adam Smith's invisible hand at work in the "gray" market. In theory, prices of goods and services are arbitrarily fixed, but these are what we would call list or sticker prices, no more than a guide intended to perplex. Modifying the price system is an even more intricate structure, unofficial but unavoidable, of discounts, surcharges, kickbacks, barter deals, and so on, and this structure is the real lifeblood of the Soviet economy.

In the 1920s and 1930s, when Soviet management was avidly copying foreign industrial systems and techniques, America was definitely Exemplar Number One, to the point of blind faith. And even in 1960, to judge by the comments of my engineering friends, the biggest name in Soviet industry, perhaps the biggest foreign name, period, was still Henry Ford. The Russians had embraced our mass-production syndrome wholeheartedly and uncritically, with enormous investments in highly specialized machinery, recruitment of armies of semiskilled labor expected to take orders and keep mouths and minds shut, and endless runs of standarized products. The Model T—any color you want as long as it's black—represented the epitome of Soviet production goals. Wedded to Russia's innate conservatism and all too readily adapted to the Russian authoritarian tradition, these imported ideas quickly hardened into a dogma that has frustrated the attempts of younger engineers to seek a more flexible approach to industrialization. Besides this, the Russians also unthinkingly copied the American practice of big-farm, big-machine agriculture ("gigantism" was a Stalinist fetish). The obsession with horizon-to-horizon plowing knocked flat proposals to prevent soil erosion, and the inevitable result has been a disastrous loss of the Soviet Union's greatest geological resource, its best farm land. Many of the Russian complaints I heard had familiar American echoes.

On a polar expedition, as with kamikaze pilots, motivation is taken for granted. But back at home, I was made to understand, the labor problem was fundamental—and has been so since the Russian revolution, when "worker control" was deliberately subverted by both Communists and counterrevolutionaries to make it appear impracticable. One tenet of socialism is uncomfortably applicable in the Soviet Union. In describing the intrinsic superiority of free over slave labor, Karl Marx pointed out that the worker who feels that he is treated as a mere instrument of production will assert his indomitable humanity by reacting destructively against the instruments he is forced to use. The coercive Soviet system, in which employees are not even allowed to go on strike, inevitably brings this principle into play. Soviet workers may not be outright Luddites, but they have ways to achieve the same effect without smashing machinery.

Like the cost of maintaining our polar outpost against the elements, the price of a functioning industrial civilization is eternal diligence. Its inherent tendency to lapse into a state of disorder—to increase its entropy, so to speak—can be arrested only by an unending, demanding, and intelligent struggle. Hence it is not necessary to sabotage the system actively to bring it to its knees. You can just "let it be." This "workers' opposition," as it was called in the 1920s, is (to steal a phrase from old Bolshevik Trotsky) in "permanent revolution," and it uses a natural law: the Second Law of Thermodynamics preempts any Kremlin *ukaz* (decree).

The resistance of the working class, which shows up in such industrial deficiencies as low productivity, poor quality of goods, and huge backlogs of unfinished projects, is not without its psychological costs. There is a "Bridge on the River Kwai" conflict between the natural desire to do a good job—and Russians don't lack this feeling—and the basic impulse to thwart the Enemy, who in this case is (as Walt Kelly put it) "us"—that is, other Russians.

At the other end of the social scale, the apex of the class system, is the *Nomenklatura* or list of names; the names of the elect, the oligarchy. It is also the name of the game, the pot of gold for the upwardly mobile. The *Nomenklatura*, as described to me, sounded analagous to the table of ranks established by Peter the Great to define the Czarist nobility. In another sense, it can be viewed as the register of effective owners, the stockholders in what amounts to a holding company covering the thousands of business enterprises that make up the Soviet economy. These fortunate few are entitled to the profits, the dividends, which accrue largely in the guise of special privileges and payments in kind. The perquisites that I heard the most about were the dachas (which in this context were really villas), special discount stores stocked with luxury goods unobtainable elsewhere, limousine services, exclusive vacation resorts, sumptuous hunting and fishing clubs, and personal servants. Like everything else in this inordinately pecuniary culture, membership in the *Nomenklatura* is for sale to the highest bidder—there is even a sort of informal stock market, just as there is for lucrative state positions. This subject didn't exist at all as far as the official media were concerned, but it was evidently a major topic of conversation. However, among the workers the usual expression was not *Nomenklatura* but *Razboiniki*—robbers.

The social origins of the personages in the ruling circles, as claimed in their official biographies, were frequently the targets of ridicule. It is well known that Lenin's father was a Czarist nobleman, and from what I heard, this was far from the exceptional instance it is usually made out to be. The perception is that a lot more continuity exists between old and new ruling classes than has been admitted in the U.S.S.R. or suspected in the West. A fairly typical remark was, "If you really believe that all those high party characters are the sons of workers and peasants, you'll believe the story we tell our children about babies coming from cabbages!"

The people of the Soviet Union have been the prime victims of two of the most diabolical figures in history, Adolf Hitler and Josef Vissarionovich Stalin. In 1960 Hitler had been dead for fifteen years and Stalin for seven, but their ghosts hovered over the land and the survivors like poisonous clouds. The visitation of one such tormentor in ten centuries would be a horrible enough fate for any nation, but to have been whip-sawed by two such scourges in a single generation was a curse of cosmic proportions. To a people of philosophical and theological bent like the Russians, this dual cataclysm posed soul-searching questions about the nature of absolute evil: How could it have happened? Why us, of all people? Did He who made the Lamb make Josef Vissarionovich?

There was some reluctance at first on the part of my companions to talk about Stalin and his cult of personality. The tyrant's body still reposed in the Lenin Mausoleum and was not moved to a more modest site until the following year. But when they did talk it was clear that Stalin had been an enemy of the people in the literal meaning of that much-abused expression. He was a man of total malevolence, a dedicated sadist, who trusted no motives except greed and the lust for power. The evil official acts of his era were invariably venal: the system of forced labor camps was, above all, a profit-making enterprise that could well have been called "Gulag, Inc." Nobody in a position of authority was even remotely trying to build a brave new world. The ends, the means, and the actors were alike malign. Stalin and his henchmen consciously and maliciously created an "ill-fare state," which sought the greatest misery for the greatest number, and I heard nothing to suggest that they ever intended anything else.

My Russian friends differed in their opinions about Stalin. The differences in this case, however, did not concern his guilt or innocence, only the degree of his guilt. A few party and Komsomol types tried to put much of the onus on underlings—as in Czarist times, harsh rule was not attributed to the "little father" himself, but to his corrupt agents. They blamed the late security boss, Lavrenti P. Beria (a universally and apparently deservedly despised man), for domestic repression and the former foreign minister Vyacheslav M. Molotov (now relegated to minor posts) for foreign policy "mistakes" (like the Nazi-Soviet pact in 1939), as if the leader who claimed omniscience didn't know what was going on. Stalin's apologists preferred to credit him with such "good works" as industrialization and wartime leadership while minimizing his responsibility for the cruel methods, disastrous blunders, and terrible human costs that attended even these achievements. Not unexpectedly, those who wanted to whitewash Stalin also admired those ruthless movers and shakers of yore, Ivan the Terrible (Stalin's personal hero and role model), and Peter the Great.

The workers, however, tended not to beat around the bush. To them Stalin was, quite simply, the personification of the counterrevolution: the bloody sword of a new exploiting class and the final liquidator of the proletarian movement. As they told it, the biggest obstacle to Stalin's brutal policies had been the opposition of those who thought that socialism meant equality, cooperation, internationalism, and a voice for the workers in their own destiny (in other words, the sort of do-gooders Stalin hated). These people had no place in the new order of extreme inequality, intense competition (labelled "emulation"), national chauvinism, and authoritarian management that the despot deemed essential for the rapid accumulation of industrial capital. Nevertheless, I was assured that although Stalin's will had triumphed temporarily, the old revolutionary values had survived. Some even thought that despite the iron heel of the entrenched oligarchy, the workers would ultimately prevail.

Notwithstanding all the difficulties, many worthwhile things were accomplished even during the reign of Stalin. People motivated by the ideals of the lost revolution, a sense of duty to their countrymen, or simply personal integrity continued to serve their fellows in many fields of endeavor. Though Soviet science was presided over by destructive charlatans like the agricultural czar Trofim D. Lysenko, honest researchers worked quietly at real science in the back rooms of laboratories, often at the risk not only of their jobs, but of their lives. The unheralded deeds of this scientific underground constitute one of the most inspiring chapters in the history of the human quest for knowledge. As Galileo proved, the earth still moves, despite the Inquisition.

World War II had been the greatest event in the lives of my companions, and I heard countless stories about it. Those who were my own age, the "younger-brother" generation, remembered the war as a desperate, exhausting, all-out struggle to supply the armed forces, while at the front the men a few years older had faced an appallingly high risk of death or dismemberment. It was not uncommon to see a young man who had gray hair as a result of wartime malnutrition. Many had worked in munitions factories from an early age, since this was the only way to obtain adequate rations—when they were available at all—for their families. Sometimes my friends would engage in a macabre version of "Can you top this?" arguing about where conditions had been the harshest: at the front, in one of the cities under siege (Leningrad, Odessa, Sebastopol), in the villages under enemy occupation. With all due respect to the embattled soldiers and the besieged citizens, I think the villages took the unenviable "prize."

Loss of life in the "Great Fatherland War," as the Soviet-Nazi phase of World War II is officially called, was colossal. At the start of Operation Barbarossa, Reichsführer S.S. Heinrich Himmler declared that thirty *million* people had to be liquidated in the east to secure German lebensraum. In the event, the Nazis killed even more. The consensus among the veterans I talked to was that a minimum of one-sixth of the prewar Soviet population (about two hundred million) perished between 1941 and 1945. Soldiers' deaths—killed in action, died of wounds, deliberately exterminated as prisoners of war—while enormous, were far surpassed by civilian fatalities.

The Nazi-occupied territory was one vast charnel house. The first mass killings involved people of "racial," political, and cultural categories specifically marked for extinction: Jews, Gypsies, Communists, Komsomols, intellectuals. Then came the victims of forced labor: death by starvation, disease, and exposure in a land the invaders had stripped of food, medicines, doctors, and shelter. Hostages were indiscriminately executed in reprisal for resistance to the occupying authorities. Great numbers of innocent people were caught in depopulation sweeps carried out to drain areas of antifascist guerillas. And when they at last retreated, the Nazis embraced a policy of leaving nothing alive or standing for the victors to liberate.

One little-noted aspect of the war on the eastern front that was vividly described to me was the Luftwaffe's incendiary bombing campaign. By the 1940s the burgeoning Soviet cities were ringed by flimsy wooden shantytowns that housed industrial workers. These slums were highly flammable targets for Hermann Goering's raiders, and the firestorms at Kiev and Stalingrad (now Volgograd) were as devastating as any in the entire war.

The impact of the war on the Russian people and the skin-of-our-teeth state of mind that it produced are difficult for the people of a sheltered country like the United States to understand. Certainly the national paranoia for which Russians have long been notorious was heightened. The conflict generated a combination of national and "racial" animosities and included the worst features of both. The atrocities of the eastern front relegate the practices of barbarous tribes to peccadilloes. For Russia, defeat would have meant obliteration as a nation and a culture, the extermination of "anyone who looks sideways" (a slogan attributed to Goering), and enslavement of the remainder as "subhumans." That was the future Adolf Hitler had planned for the conquered people of the east, and it was realized as far as possible in the occupied territory. Once this nightmare began to be real, Russians had no choice but to conclude that, bad as Stalinism was, Hitler's program operated at an even deeper level of Hell.

In this grim struggle there was none of the fraternization across the trenches that occasionally lightened the agony of the First World War, when enemies sometimes called a brief truce and got together to celebrate common holidays. The only incident of chivalrous behavior that I heard about in our many long discussions of the war took place during the fighting in the Caucasus Mountains in the fall of 1942, when the Wehrmacht was making its ambitious drive for the Middle Eastern oilfields. At one point, Russian and German alpine troops engaged in a battle among the peaks, and some of the German soldiers became trapped in a cul-de-sac. Desperately seeking an escape route, they were caught on an exposed ledge in the face of a blizzard, but were rescued—and captured—by the Russians. Afterward, around a campfire, the traditional camaraderie of mountaineers briefly asserted itself in the middle of mortal combat, like a summit piercing the clouds, and captors and captives passed around vodka and schnapps while they talked about their prewar climbing experiences.

One of my companions had served through the entire war and fought in several of the most famous battles. He was one of the few survivors among those first called to duty. His opinions were pretty much what might be called the establishment line, but they were tempered by the honesty and realism I almost invariably found among our many combat veterans. What follows is the gist of a talk I had with this former Red Army officer, who had a keen sense of history.

DEWART: The Battle of Stalingrad still fascinates us in the West. How did you Russians really manage to win it?

RUSSIAN VETERAN: Well, as Napoleon said, the closer you look at a battle, the less brilliant seems the victory and the less excusable the defeat. Basically, we just made fewer mistakes than the fascists did. They were still overconfident at that stage because of their early victories, and that made them careless. We had learned the hard way that a ruined city makes a splendid fortress, and we became masters of house-to-house fighting. The form of combat was in our favor, too—it wasn't so much a grand battle of divisions and corps, where German tactics were admittedly superior, but a disorganized struggle of individuals and small units, and that was our strength. Above all, it was a defensive fight on our own sacred soil that brought out the best qualities of our soldiers: their tenacity, toughness, and ability to improvise.

DEWART: How would you rank it with the other decisive battles?

RUSSIAN VETERAN: The defense of Moscow in 1941 showed that we could survive, Stalingrad in 1942 showed that we *could* win, and Kursk, in the summer of 1943, showed that we *would* win. We Russians emphasize the importance of the battle of the Kursk Salient. It was the greatest tank battle in history, and we have an obsession with armor.

DEWART: How would you rate your weapons versus theirs?

RUSSIAN VETERAN: The advantage went back and forth; we had some surprises for them and they had some for us. But remember, the human factor was decisive even there. Our war industry produced good weapons then because it was life or death for our whole people, the defense of our homes. But it took us a long time to learn to use our weapons as effectively as the fascists did. They were terribly strong, and there is no doubt that they had marvelous discipline, staff work, technical competence, and leadership. We had enormous respect for them as professional soldiers.

DEWART: Were you aware of American assistance during the war?

RUSSIAN VETERAN: Of course; many of our people survived only because of the food and medicine you sent us. We will always be grateful for that.

DEWART: What about the war matériel we provided?

RUSSIAN VETERAN: Frankly, I don't think the armaments you supplied had very much effect at the front. But the trucks and jeeps and radio equipment and transport planes were a great help in our logistics and communications. And the icebreakers you lent us helped keep our vital sealanes open.

DEWART: Yes, I sailed on one of those ships during the IGY. One of our officers had taken her back from you people at the end of the war. He said you turned her over in beautiful condition.

RUSSIAN VETERAN: Well, we were very appreciative. Not that we couldn't have won the war without you and the British, but it would certainly have taken a lot more time and cost us many more lives.

DEWART: Was the famous Russian winter an effective ally for you?

RUSSIAN VETERAN: It surely was, especially that first winter, when the fascists were not nearly so well prepared for cold-weather operations as we were—that fatal overconfidence again. But besides the cold, there were also the sudden thaws. The blitzkrieg bogged down in our moat of mud. The primitive state of our roads helped, too. The fascists must have looked at their maps and thought we had autobahns, but they were lucky to find cowpaths. They soon learned a good lesson: don't take anything for granted about Russia. By the way, our roads are still atrocious.

DEWART: When your forces finally got to Germany, they treated the people there very badly, didn't they?

RUSSIAN VETERAN: That's true; a lot of things happened that stained the honor of the Red Army. Some of our soldiers had built up a lot of hatred, and vengeance is not a pretty emotion. It is, in fact, reactionary, because it focuses morbidly on the past. Still, overall, when you

consider the dreadful things it did, Germany got off lightly. And remember, at the end the S.S. was starting to do to its own people what
it had done to us. We put a stop to them.

DEWART: Do you think that you should have entered the war
against Japan?

RUSSIAN VETERAN: No. Who needed another war when we were already completely exhausted? That effort set us back years when we
were in desperate shape. It was a business deal all around. The West
bought an ally, and Stalin bought some more territory, and the price
was Russian blood. And then it turned out that you didn't need us
after all.

DEWART: What are your thoughts on the war in the Pacific?

RUSSIAN VETERAN: A bathtub war; you know, we think of it as children playing with toy boats. (I visibly bristled at this—I had friends in
the Seabees and an uncle who had spent a year in New Guinea.) Excuse me, I didn't mean to belittle your victory. Frankly, we Russians,
as a great land power, don't take naval warfare seriously enough.

DEWART: Without command of the sea, the Allies couldn't have
provided war materials for you or invaded Europe and created the
Second Front that you wanted so much.

RUSSIAN VETERAN: Amphibious operations on that scale are really
beyond our comprehension. But we do wish it had come a lot sooner.

DEWART: That's ironic. If the Allies had been able to open the Second Front sooner, when your armies were still far to the east, Russian
might not now control so much of Europe.

RUSSIAN VETERAN: Yes, there is often irony in war and politics. In
the First World War (my father was in that one) the Western powers
used our troops as cannon fodder against the German army, but that
only helped bring on the revolution, which they dreaded even more
than the Kaiser. Then our friend Churchill tried to strangle the revolution at birth by invading and starving us, but that only hammered
Russian into an iron dictatorship. And who would have guessed, in
the Second World War we saved dear Churchill from the fascists.

DEWART: What is your opinion of Winston Churchill's wartime
role?

RUSSIAN VETERAN: First, last, and always, he was an imperialist. But
he really hated Hitler, and you have to admire his courage and
persistence.

DEWART: What is your assessment of Stalin, militarily, that is?

(There was the usual pause at this topic.) Stalin created a ruinous climate of suspicion. The surest way to make a man disloyal is to distrust him, and Stalin distrusted everybody. The purges before the war gravely weakened our forces, and the surprise at the start of the war was inexcusable—it was your Pearl Harbor many times over. After that, to give the devil his due, he settled down and gave us strong— but quite ruthless—leadership.

DEWART: How about Franklin Roosevelt?

RUSSIAN VETERAN: Roosevelt was a very good man; he helped us immeasurably in the war, and we know that he sincerely wanted international cooperation in the postwar world.

DEWART: What about Harry Truman?

RUSSIAN VETERAN: A bad man. He wanted to let the fascists and us destroy each other, regardless of how many innocent people died. And he cut off lend-lease right after V-E day, when our need was still great. Wasn't Truman a member of the Ku Klux Klan?

DEWART: No. What do you think of President Eisenhower? You don't have to be diplomatic.

RUSSIAN VETERAN: Oh, we like and admire the old general very much. After all, we were comrades-in-arms. We feel that he is the typical American: friendly, generous, and well-intentioned. But there are wicked men around him and evil influences at work on him.

DEWART: What do you think about our prospects for peace in the future?

RUSSIAN VETERAN: There has been so much killing that I believe our government will be very reluctant for Russian blood to be shed in any foreign adventures for a long time; there is a sort of social compact to that effect. The common people are overwhelmingly and passionately devoted to peace. But the proletariat doesn't dictate to anyone here, and generals—yours as well as ours—get restless. Remember what Napoleon said: You can do many things with bayonets, but you cannot sit on them.

The immediate postwar period brought nearly as much misery as the war had to the people of the Soviet Union. The formal termination of hostilities did not end the horrible famine conditions, accompanied by deadly epidemics, in western Russia and the Ukraine, where the Nazi devastation had left the economic structure in ruins. It was also the "time of the amputees," when millions of crippled veterans could be reduced to begging on street corners. For security reasons, the government downplayed the grim conditions, just as it minimized wartime losses. The human costs of the war's aftereffects are incalculable.

In many regions anarchy prevailed. Banditry and guerrilla warfare were rife, as partisan bands refused to give up their lawless ways, separatist militants took advantage of the disorder to rebel, and local politicos set themselves up as robber barons. In the cities gangs of orphaned youths and embittered ex-soldiers made the streets unsafe. The chaos was aggravated by "werewolf" agents and their collaborators, who had been left behind like viruses by the invaders. Martial law remained in effect in some areas until 1952, and only then was the war really over for the Soviet people.

It was the age of the *Blat*—fixers, influence peddlers, speculators. The black market flourished, and organized crime and official corruption were rampant. The ordinary citizen had to hustle just to survive. Over the suffering country moved the relentless Stalin and his rapacious henchman Beria, enforcing their own brand of order with a rod of steel. Only the corrupt, cynical, and opportunistic were suitable for the dictator's purposes, and only they were promoted to positions of authority. The corruption inevitably became institutionalized. I had to bear in mind that these terrible times were very fresh in the memories of my companions.

7

Explorations of the Mind

> Science and art belong to the whole world, and before
> them vanish the boundaries of nationality.
> —*Johann Wolfgang von Goethe*

Nationalism is one of those two-edged topics that make conversations with Russians so interesting. Khrushchev had begun one of the periodic Russification drives in September 1959, and while Russian "patriotism" was in, the "nationalism" of the other ethnic groups in the empire was definitely out. This was a very touchy matter because of the great diversity of peoples involved. Sharp regional divisions exist even within the dominant groups, the Great Russians and their reluctant junior partners, the Ukrainians (it was fairly typical that our leader, Korotkevich, was a Russian, and his deputy, Matveychuk, was a Ukrainian). The sheer bulk of the country encourages disunity, especially in view of the poor transportation and communications. Russian nationalism and polar exploration have been closely intertwined at least since Peter the Great sent Vitus Bering out on the Great Northern Expedition in 1725. The history of our logistical support agency, the Northern Sea Route Administration, which was founded in 1932, was no exception. Stalin seized upon an incident that occurred in the Arctic in 1934 to focus renewed emphasis on national consciousness, one of his major policies.

Otto J. Schmidt, the first director of Glavsevmorput, was commanding the icebreaking cargo ship *Chelyuskin* (named for an early explorer) on a research voyage off the coast of Siberia when it became beset in the pack near Bering Strait. The *Chelyuskin* sank, but the survivors succeeded in establishing a safe camp and landing strip on the sea ice and were evacuated without loss of life by an airlift organized by Ivan Papanin. Schmidt, Papanin, and the others were given a triumphal reception in Moscow that was turned into a chauvinistic extravaganza. Old words like *rodina* (native land) and *otechestvo* (fatherland) were repopularized, and the *Chelyuskin* affair marked a giant step in the postrevolutionary revival of patriotic sentiment. At that time, historians who had taken the Marxist standpoint of criticizing Czarist imperialism suddenly disappeared.

Russians tend to have stereotyped views of themselves and of other nationalities. They see their own country as a simple, guileless character, a Li'l Abner type who is constantly being conned and defrauded by sinister schemers until he finally rises in righteous wrath and smites them. At the same time, they are anxious that they may be disliked and sneered at by others and sensitive about being considered *bezkulturnyy* (uncultured or uncouth). They are suspicious even of those neighbors who are (officially) "friends." I detected an echo of the resentment one occasionally finds in Western Europe: that those vanquished in the last war are sometimes better off than the victors. The Russians had an almost Romanov-like attitude toward Eastern Europe. If Russian hegemony did not exist there, something else would fill the vacuum, and that something else might be dangerous to them. But those small nations that have stood up to them seem to have earned their respect, for I heard admiration expressed for Hungarians, Yugoslavs, and Finns (the last were referred to as "tough people"). While some stoutly maintained that the satellite countries were fully independent, they also made it clear that Russia would never again let this strategic region, this "springboard for aggression," fall into unfriendly hands. This is one of the deepest scars of the war.

Anti-Semitism is an old story in the Russian empire, and it was still being used as a scapegoat for social deficiencies. At the time this took the form of selective prosecution of "economic crimes," by which is meant financial finagling that is the Russian national pastime and is generally condoned. Soviet drives against corruption consist entirely of rounding up the usual suspects, who are usually Jewish, Armenian, Azerbaijani, or Georgian. The few ethnic Russians roped in are those who neglected to pay their bribes. The arrangement is familiar to anyone who has lived under a corrupt political machine.

I heard few anti-Semitic remarks. Traditional anti-Jewish sentiment had apparently been muted by popular knowledge of Nazi victimization of the Jews and the magnificent contribution that surviving Jews had made to the Soviet war effort. These facts were ignored, however, by the official media, a situation that did not become a public issue until Yevgeny Yevtushenko published his poetic bombshell, "Babi Yar," in 1962.

You do hear some ethnic humor while sitting around the camp stove, but none of it is awfully malicious. I heard Jewish jokes, Armenian jokes, Polish jokes, and Russian jokes. Germans are not thought to be funny, however, nor are Turks, the hereditary foe. Belorussians (White Russians) are the butt of rustic, hayseed-type humor. I heard a good deal about the poverty of Belorussia, and was struck years later by how closely what I had learned resembled the disillusioned memoirs of a notorious fellow who was living in the Belorussian capital of Minsk while I was at Mirnyy—Lee Harvey Oswald.

Difficulties between Russia and China were just beginning to surface in 1960, and the official Soviet attitude was still that an unbreakable bond existed between the two nations. Not until technical assistance was abruptly withdrawn from China on July 17 was any problem admitted by our prime news source, Radio Moscow. This was a shock to those who had been discounting the reports of Sino-Soviet tension from the BBC. My colleagues, however, had exhibited an ambivalent attitude toward their giant neighbor to the east long before that. When I first inquired about relations with China, they were described as "fraternal," and I heard the expected praise for the Chinese revolution and the mandatory expressions of respect for the Chinese people. One party man who had been to China on a technical aid mission described with awe how he was strolling through a park in

Peking when the ubiquitous loudspeakers came on with a speech by one of the bigwigs. All the people in the park immediately ceased what they were doing to listen—old men stopped talking, children stopped playing, "My God, even the babies stopped crying! Can you imagine that in Russia? Here some idiot always blows his nose at the key word in a speech. They have what we need, discipline."

A professor from Leningrad who had taught Chinese exchange students was enthusiastic in his praise of their diligence and serious attitudes. He compared them favorably with his feckless Russian students: "With the Chinese it was work, work, work; with the Russians it was play, chase girls, drink vodka!" Some of the Komsomols saw the Chinese revolution as purer and more humane than the Russian, and thought that they might have something to learn from it. Serious dissension between the two "progressive" powers was unthinkable.

But then there was the case of the boned chicken. We had received some of our supplies from the fraternal countries of what was then called the Soviet Bloc. These imports included excellent beer from Czechoslovakia, delicious strawberries from Bulgaria, and some canned chicken from the People's Republic of China. The label read "bones removed." We opened one of the cans at a party and hungrily dug into the tempting white chicken meat, only to discover that it was merely a layer about half an inch deep. The rest of the large can contained nothing but greasy bones. The company erupted with laughter and such derisive comments as:

"Some of these bones aren't even chicken bones!"

"Well, we can always make soup out of it!"

"Boned chicken, indeed! That's just about what we can expect from our beloved Chinese comrades."

I probed the question a little further and was surprised to find that even in that period of outward friendship it was common knowledge, backed up by descriptions by those who had been there, that the border between Russia and China was the most heavily guarded in the world. Fear for the security of that immense, sparsely populated treasure chest, Siberia, was obvious and not unlike concern I had found among Australians, who are also uneasily thin on a vast expanse of ground. I also detected a certain disquiet about what my friends called "great-power chauvinism" and the "cult of personality" in China. It takes a good deal of gall for either Russians or Americans to accuse anybody else of being chauvinistic, but the Stalinist cult was a recent and very harrowing memory for the Russian people, and the ominous similarities in Maoism understandably raised their hackles. Interestingly, they had no doubt at all that Stalin had engineered the Korean War in order to bring the U.S. and China into conflict.

Was racial antagonism a factor in the suspicious attitude toward China? It's a tricky question. "Race" is very much in the eye of the beholder. Some Russians consider Germans another race, while fellow Russians with strongly Mongolian features are not. We should remember that in Russia people of the same race—and the same color, nationality, language, religion, and culture—have enslaved each other for centuries. I heard nothing to suggest that the Sino-Soviet conflict was anything other than the traditional competition between two imperial dynasties for dominance over the Eurasian land mass. The crux was not race or ideology, but real estate.

Incidentally, I was mildly surprised that nobody came on very strong about America's grievous racial problems, since it was in 1960 that sit-ins at segregated lunch counters began in the south. The stopover in Capetown had been a real eye-opener on race relations for my companions; they had read about such things as apartheid, of course, but Russians don't believe much of what they see in their newspapers. Now they, and in particular one man of Tartar ancestry who was refused service in a public accommodation, could observe with their own eyes that what they had read was not just propaganda. But I heard a forthright admission about this situation that ran: "We Russians are no angels. If we had black people in our country, we would probably discriminate against them, too."

One thing that had stuck in my mind since I had first joined the Russians was the small crowd of people who had come to the dock and watched quietly when the *Kooperatsiya* departed from Capetown. When I asked, "Who were those people at wharfside? Don't tell me you guys have fans even in South Africa?" I got the response, "Ah, yes, those people were Russians—old Russians. They are the émigrés, or descendants of the émigrés, who fled from Russia during and after the revolution. But they still carry a part of Russia within themselves. We see people like these at every port, in every country. They know when every Soviet ship is due, and they meet it and try to talk to us.

"Of course, we are warned against these people, but that is

foolish—they are not our enemies any more. They just want to buy us a drink, talk with us about the homeland, have some human contact with anyone who is from what is still 'Holy Russia' to them. It is strange and a little sad. The younger ones have never even been to Russia, but they are so very Russian, in an antiquated way. They seem like characters in an old movie. It is very touching for us, too. Perhaps only another Slav could understand."

Once when I was sitting in a sidewalk cafe in the cosmopolitan King's Cross district of Sydney, I overheard a couple of "New Australians" who had been refugees from central Europe discussing a certain pair of nationalities:

"The Russians and Americans are not bad people basically, but they are like children, they are ruled by impulse."

"How true; I saw it in the war. One moment they will give their last crust of bread to a hungry child, and the next they will shoot you for the gold in your teeth."

Whether or not this is a fair assessment, I couldn't help thinking of the early nineteenth-century traveler's description of the American frontiersman, in whose pockets could be found a book of poems, a Bowie knife, an affectionate letter to his daughter, and a scheme to defraud his neighbor of his farm. The national characters of America and Russia share strong similarities, and I think they go deeper than just having some of the same inconsistencies. The Russians generally expressed a warm kinship and admiration for America and its people; as far as I could tell, a decade and a half of total saturation in often virulent anti-American propaganda had produced virtually no effect. Especially appealing to them in the American myth was the concept of the Westerner, the man of action, strong, independent, and free. Some made a romantic association of this ideal type with the Cossacks of the past and the new pioneers in Siberia. Floating down the Volga on a raft à la Huckleberry Finn is a fantasy of many Russian youths. It was immensely encouraging to me to find that freedom is like what O. Henry said about wealth: you don't have to possess it to understand it.

When the United States was criticized, it tended to be what a star performer can expect if he puts on a pedestrian performance—excellence is not only expected but demanded. The double standard, after all, can be the sincerest form of compliment. My experience makes me think that the Russian people like Americans better than they like any of their own allies. They probably like us better than our own allies do.

Russians and Americans (and, I suppose, everyone else) have the same nationalistic quirk: even though at home we know what rascally crooks our politicians are, we automatically assume that they are the souls of honor when dealing with foreigners. After a while, though, we overcame this I-can-whip-my-kids-but-don't-you-touch-them syndrome and could talk disinterestedly about international politics. On an expedition a new sense of loyalty puts old thought patterns in a new perspective and can break down preconceptions and prejudices.

To a man, the Russians I talked to favored closer relations— "peaceful coexistence"—with the United States (the word *détente* was not yet in fashion). Just what this meant, aside from not shooting at each other, was not always so clear. Many seemed to think of it largely in terms of increased commerce between the two nations. Despite their reputation for hardheaded pragmatism, some of the Russians shared the liberal illusions that many in the West have about "peaceful trade." I was a bit surprised and irritated to hear such simpering euphemisms as "trading partners" when what was meant was "cut-throat competitors." They were rather jarred when I rudely thrust the platitudes aside and injected a note of cynicism: "What's so peaceful about trade? It's a struggle, a cause of contention, a means of overmastering. Don't worry about ideology—wars are fought over trade and turf. Haven't you guys ever been in a competitive business?" A fellow geologist nodded gravely and then enumerated the "issues" involved in the fighting that was then going on in central Africa: uranium, copper, cobalt, manganese, tin, diamonds.

My friends were fully aware of the higher living standard in America, though they did not have much of an idea of such welfare state measures as social security and unemployment insurance. In discussing them I encountered some amusingly familiar attitudes from party hard-liners: "What, you pay people for not working? Why would anyone work, then?"

The young social dropouts of that time, the beatniks, were well known, probably because of Nikita Khrushchev's widely publicized scorn. They were universally regarded with contempt and an amazing amount of hostility as drones and parasites.

To the party members, democracy plus welfare spending was a formula for fiscal irresponsibility. For example, they would say, "If you let the people decide these things, they will just vote themselves bigger and bigger benefits and smaller and smaller taxes until the state goes bankrupt."

The Sunday *New York Times* was a real wonder to them. They simply didn't know what to make of a publication of such caliber and dimensions. The sheer technical achievement it represented aroused their admiration, but particularly fascinating for them was the advertising, and especially the classified ads. From used cars to sybaritic luxury items, it displayed a kaleidoscope of everything that they applauded or disapproved in America. They were also amused by the prices and commented, "We don't have prices like those in the Soviet Union." "What do you mean, so high, so low?" "No, I mean prices like $3.98 and $12.95. Our published prices are always round numbers!"

The Russians were also quite interested in my sample copies of the small-town weekly newspapers that my parents were printing in California. They were astonished at the open criticism of the government in the editorial column in a legal publication. This was something they could see only in *Samizdat*. The "personal" items about the doings of local citizens were also an unfamiliar aspect of journalism to them. My plugs for freedom of the press, backed by quotations from Horace Greeley and his sometime columnist Karl Marx, were eagerly accepted by some, but party members stonewalled the idea.

Samizdat, by the way, is another of those extraordinary Russian paradoxes. It is the most vibrant, aggressive, irreverent press in the world, and it is all-pervasive, but it is also illegal. Russia has an incredibly "free" press, but it is also "unfree." Only mindless hacks read the official press, but in those days it wasn't even trying to compete.

My companions were intrigued by the "American Way of Life" (they were quite familiar with the phrase), and their reactions to my autobiographical anecdotes frequently told me a great deal about their own lives. They would sometimes express amazement at things I considered unremarkable. For example, I told them about running a

gas station at the age of sixteen and being entrusted with all the sales
responsibilities, including carrying the day's receipts home with me
from the night shift. This mundane account of small-town life was
greeted with the looks customarily reserved for bragging fishermen.
It wasn't until they described in detail the cumbersome, suspicious,
and demeaning retail system they were accustomed to that I fully
understood their skepticism about an ordinary worker, especially one
so young, enjoying even a minimal degree of trust and autonomy
from higher-ups.

They were amused by my teenage commercial ventures, such as
recycling beer bottles from our hard-drinking neighborhood back to
the saloons for the deposit money, selling produce from my truck
farm on a vacant lot, peddling sawmill waste for kindling wood to
owners of coal-burning furnaces, and trapping rabbits for the state
game commission. This is the sort of thing that Russian kids do, too,
to make some money. The availability of cheap secondhand automo-
biles, however, was astounding to them, and the access to firearms
was simply beyond their ken.

Ths Russian way is to start with a sweeping generalization and then
make exceptions to it until, quite often, the exceptions become the
rule. Exemptions and deferments from military service were many,
and few of the technical personnel in my age bracket had served in
their armed forces. Similarly, one could get around the supposedly
mandatory two-year posting to an assigned job that followed gradua-
tion from a university in any number of ways.

Although several of my friends were surprisingly well informed
about California, aside from the state of Texas and the cities of New
York and Washington they had a pretty hazy conception of the rest of
the United States. Nevertheless, they certainly knew more about
America than almost any American I've talked to knows about Russia. They greatly envied us our geographical situation, including both
our isolation from other big powers and our southerly location. To
Russians, the whole United States, except Alaska, is in the sun belt:
Tashkent, which is synonymous with heat, has about the same latitude as Chicago.

They were keenly aware of the glamor of Hollywood, and some of
the younger men were clearly disappointed that I was not able to tell
them more about current stars and scandals. Russians are always

impressed by technical competence, and they were unstinting in their praise of American motion pictures as productions, regardless of what they may have thought about the content. Walt Disney was a special hero to them, and I was reproved, half-seriously, because Khrushchev had not been allowed to make a pilgrimage to Disneyland on his trip to southern California.

Soviet citizens are justly notorious for their drab and ill-cut clothing; it may have been making a virtue of a necessity, but lack of style seemed almost to be a matter of principle to them. The Arctic Institute of North America had issued me two colorful lumberjack shirts, one checked black and red, the other black and green. They were standard items, and I thought nothing of them. However, when I first appeared in one of them, the garment provoked murmurs of disapproval: "In Russia, men do not wear such bright colors" ("*V Rossii*"—"in Russia"—always preceded moralizing strictures of this kind). I explained that these shirts were traditionally worn by Canadian loggers, whose machismo could hardly be doubted. This mollified them—after all, Canadians were a northern people, too—but they still considered the offending garb to be outlandish, an aberration permitted only to a foreign guest. This incident, like the controversy over the growing of beards, illustrates a potent factor in Russian life: the force of informal public opinion, which is often directed against any exhibition of nonconformism. Russians can be dreadful nags and scolds, all the time meaning it sincerely for your own good. It is no accident that the *babuskha* (grandmother) is such a prominent figure in Russian folklore.

Though Soviet society is officially quite puritanical, the old moral standards were visibly eroding, especially among the city-dwellers. In the backwoods, religious villages the formal prudery of the party line was best in tune with popular culture. Even among urbanites, however, the sexual double standard was fully developed. Fairly typical was a story I heard about a female crew member who became pregnant on one of the expedition cruises. Her name and offense were posted prominently on the ship's bulletin board, just like in the old Massachusetts Bay Colony. Nothing was said about the man in the affair.

The fact that women hold about half the jobs in the Soviet Union is accepted as socially just, though these jobs are largely the most menial. Of course, a working wife is usually necessary for the typically straitened family budget. At the same time, the rare wife who doesn't have to work is an elegant status symbol for the well-to-do husband. When it came to choosing a mate, old-fashioned girls seemed to be preferred by my sample of Soviet manhood. While we were listening to the Olympic Games over Radio Moscow we heard an interview with a couple of female athletes from the Soviet Union. The first one sounded sweet and shy, and her demeanor was warmly approved by our circle. The second one was bold and outspoken, and one of the group said flatly, "We don't like that kind of girl." There were murmurs of assent from the others.

The Russians took an avid interest in the presidential campaign of 1960, as they were well aware of the importance that American politics could have for them, and I tried to explain the proceedings as best I could. The relationship of the branches of government, the electoral system, the parties, and the primaries were understood only vaguely and in part by my hosts, and elucidating them put unanticipated demands on my knowledge of political science. "Know thyself—and thy country" is a good rule for anyone embarking on a venture like mine.

Actually, personality turned out to be more important than technics to most of the election watchers. My companions tended to form snap judgments of the various primary contenders. Nelson Rockefeller, revealingly, found favor among the party members because of his experience in managing big, complex operations and handling huge sums of money. Richard Nixon was instinctively disliked by many because he had an "unpleasant appearance." Lyndon Johnson was thought to understand the common man because he had once been a manual laborer. Adlai Stevenson, the all-around favorite, was considered to be statesmanlike, a man Khrushchev would have to respect. John F. Kennedy was considered too young for such a powerful position by many, and some didn't care for his speaking voice (maybe it was that Boston accent). The electoral process itself was taken very seriously, and it was gratifying to me that free elections— and I did not hide the flaws and limitations, whether in financing or voting rights—were widely regarded to be the sine qua non of good government by people who had never been able to participate in them.

About a quarter of the expedition personnel were members of the Communist party (KPSS), a much greater proportion than in the adult Soviet population generally. This high incidence partly reflected the relatively large number of university graduates and senior functionaries present. Generally speaking, the higher you go in the managerial hierarchy, the greater the percentage of party members. The party bears a distinct resemblance to the stereotypical U.S. "establishment": white, male, middle-aged, upper income, college educated. The Soviet administrative structure holds few mysteries for anyone who is familiar with those collectivist entities called corporations, especially for those of us who have lived in a "company town."

The older party members were intrigued by my accounts of the union organizing drives in the New York newspaper industry in the 1930s and the simultaneous struggle against racketeering and Communist infiltration, as these events had been passed on to me by my parents, who were active participants. My stories about these bitter contests of a bygone era inevitably led to political and philosophical arguments that went on till late at night and gave me a weird feeling of déjà vu.

For many a certain moral stigma attaches to joining the party, especially among those who are sincerely socialistic in spirit. In a sense, the party is seen as a corrupt established church, a "Whore of Babylon," which is odious to the faithful. There are really two "communisms" in the Soviet Union, the hypocritical, Orwellian Communism of the party elite, and the fundamentalist communism (lower case) of the masses. Party membership is widely viewed as a vehicle for professional advancement at the expense of principle, or even as venal collaboration with "them" as against "us." I detected a community of interest between Christians and working-class communists, between those who saw Stalin as the Antichrist and those who saw him as the Antimarx.

I'm sure that my Russian friends would agree that their mother country is nothing if not paradoxical. For instance, one of the great historic heroes is the Cossack Pugachev, who headed an eighteenth-century peasant revolt against serfdom, which at that time was not far removed from plantation slavery. But an even greater hero, at least officially, is General Alexander Suvorov, the Czarist military genius who crushed Pugachev's rebellion and brought him back to the Kremlin in a cage. Still, as I pointed out to their astonishment, I have lived in a state where the birthdays of both Abraham Lincoln and

Jefferson Davis were holidays. I've read histories that called Andrew Jackson a great president, but I've also talked to Cherokees who called him a great monster. Americans can be enigmatic, too. When I told some friends with military backgrounds that in our Civil War the rank and file often elected their own officers, they were stunned. That sort of thing had been much too radical for the Bolsheviks. That common Russian character, the "doctrinaire ideologue" who runs a string of (nominally) illegal private enterprises on the side should be understandable to Americans who are familiar with Prohibition, when people would "vote Dry but drink Wet," and a certain kind of private enterprise flourished even though it was nominally illegal.

The vast so-called gray economy of private business tightly inter-locked with the pervasive bureaucratic corruption in the Soviet Union is no deep, dark secret. People spoke openly about it even then. However, it was largely ignored by western sovietologists, perhaps because simple, antiseptic, textbook models of the Soviet system were much easier to deal with than the messy, sordid, obstreperous reality. An important aspect of that reality is the maze of economic bottlenecks that are highly profitable to apparatchiki with the politi-cal clout to use them. The upshot is a social environment that is virtu-ally a hothouse for forcing mercantile mores. The "New Soviet Man" about whom propagandists used to rhapsodize is actually formed in an intensely bourgeois mold. The most characteristic social type of postrevolutionary Russia would appear to be the go-getting *tolkach* (wheeler-dealer), who resembles Pavel Ivanovich Chichikov in Niko-lai Gogol's *Dead Souls* or Milo Minderbinder in Joseph Heller's *Catch-22*. Putting it all together, I could conclude only that Voltaire's witticism about the Holy Roman Empire can be applied as well to the U.S.S.R.: it is not a union, it is not soviet, it is not socialist, and it does not consist of republics.

The Russians were fascinated by my impressions of Nikita Khrushchev—none of them had ever seen him as close up as I had. When I told them about his jokes and broad gestures, and their good-humored reception in San Francisco, there were smiles and nods. In his own country the lively chairman had the reputation of being "like an American" because of his irrepressible punning and quipping.

Khrushchev was regarded with mixed emotions. Nobody had any illusions that he was Mr. Nice Guy. He was undeniably a product of the detested Stalinist machine. Though his early career had been associated with the Ukraine, he was not an ethnic Ukrainian but a carpetbagger, and his dirty work in "pacifying" that territory before and after World War II made him about as much a Ukrainian in the eyes of the natives as General Sherman is considered a Georgian in Atlanta. Our scientists could not ignore the fact that he had kept Stalin's favorite pseudoscientist, the very symbol of quackery, Trofim Lysenko, in power. Furthermore, many were repelled by his personal crudeness, especially on the international stage, where he was the image of that mortifying stereotype, the Russian bear. On the other hand, he had exposed and denounced the crimes of Stalin, clipped the extraordinary powers and extortionate practices of the organs of state security, cut back on Russia's version of the chain-gang system, allowed living standards to rise a little, pursued the popular policy of détente with the West, and permitted a partial relaxation in the cultural sphere. In short, he was a reformer whose reforms were intended to preserve the basic structure of the oligarchic system.

The literary thaw was just getting under way at that time. I remarked to my hosts that Boris Pasternak, whose works had been suppressed in his homeland for many years, had become very popular in the United States since *Doctor Zhivago* had been published in English in 1958. Most of my circle were gratified by this information, and I was assured that much more "inflammatory" material would soon find its way past the censor's stamp. In fact, Alexander Solzhenitsyn's *A Day in the Life of Ivan Denisovich* and Yevgeny Yevtushenko's *Stalin's Heirs* appeared two years later, setting off new rounds of controversy. The hopeful ferment of fresh ideas was already very much in evidence in our discussions, but always in the background was a shade of doubt as to how long this life-enhancing springtime would last.

Russians seem to have a compulsion to wrap every aspect of human existence in a structured package of some sort, but at the same time they can act like the most disorganized people on earth. The number of institutional entities represented at Mirnyy was staggering—the party, Komsomol, the Academy of Sciences, the Ministry of Geology (imagine, I thought, a whole ministry devoted to my profession!), Glavsevmorput, Profsoyuz (our "company union"), and on and on. In some ways, it seems, the Soviet Union is almost chaotically pluralistic. The very multiplicity of such bodies affords some latitude for personal freedom if you can manage to slip through the cracks.

The world of sports is no exception in this organizational mania. In typical Russian style, a rigid, formal hierarchy of athletic recognition is in place, complete with official certification of achievement, impressive-sounding titles, and the well-known, ubiquitous medals. Beside this is, also quite typically, a very mercenary system of recruitment. Luring of talented athletes from competing teams with bribes is rampant. At the summit of athletic prowess stands the *Master Sporta* (master of sport). We had several masters on the expedition, including a cross-country skier who was good enough to have a choice between going to Antarctica and a highly rated chance at the Winter Olympic Games, which were held at Squaw Valley, California, in 1960. The travel was a potent attraction in itself, but the lure of the Great White Continent had won out: he was a true *polyarnik* at heart.

The saving grace of the Russians is their sense of humor (often, to be sure, of the gallows variety). Thus, in a mocking jab at one of their worst social problems, they have jokingly erected a pyramid of tipplers, at the apex of which stands, or rather leans, the *Master Spirta* (master of spirits).

I was a prophet with some honor among the Russians in regard to one aspect of sports. Ever since I was injured at fifteen playing football and rebuilt my body with weight training, I had been an ardent advocate of the efficacy of the big, round "iron pills" at the ends of a bar. At that time, most American coaches still scorned weightlifting both as a sport and as a training technique, but the Soviet coaching fraternity, while admitting that they originally got the idea from the Americans, had taken it up in a big way. Furthermore, weightlifting, a pretty basic kind of sport, had become widely popular among the Russians and Ukrainians, who are a pretty basic kind of people. The United States, without half trying, was still the world powerhouse of competitive lifting, but my friends predicted that the concentrated East European effort would soon surpass us, as it did. Incidentally, I was chided about the lack of capitalistic incentives for U.S. Olympic-class athletes.

Status, rank, hierarchy—these are tremendously important in the

Soviet Union, but they are in conflict with the naturally democratic tendencies that one also finds among the Russian people. This was brought home to me when I asked a man who had visited an American base what had impressed him the most about it. He replied unhesitatingly, with awe and wistfulness, "When the admiral came in late to see the cinema, nobody gave him their seat. Even the top man had to get his own chair."

I learned many things about these contradictory and sometimes maddening people, but the most important is the most obvious—that they are indeed people like ourselves, in some ways very much like ourselves. I became their confidant, heard tales of their childhood and youth, admired pictures of their wives and children, listened to their dreams and their hopes for a better future. Now I have good friends living in Moscow and Leningrad, repairing tractors on the steppes, and looking for oil in the Siberian marshes. Just as the expedition was an unforgettable part of all our lives, we each became part of one another's lives, and I will always know in a very profound sense that whatever happens to them also happens in part to me.

8

Tragedy

Down the wintry road and dreary
Flies the troika, swift, alone,
And forever tinks its weary
Tiny bell, in monotone.
                    —*Alexander Pushkin*

The Antarctic has been the scene of many tragic events in its brief but active history. In the early days of geographical discovery, men died of exhaustion and exposure as the exploring parties struggled on foot across the merciless wastes. Such was the fate of Captain Scott and his companions. In more recent times death has often come more quickly in the many aircraft and vehicle accidents and fires that have taken a heavy toll. The worst single disaster in the history of Antarctic expeditions occurred on August 3, 1960, at Mirnyy Station, when eight members of the meteorological section perished in a conflagration that destroyed their quarters during the worst storm of the year. This terrible event cast a pall of sadness over the remainder of our stay in Antarctica.

At 5:45 A.M., when it was still deep night outside, the operating engineer on duty at the central power station noticed that there had been a failure in the electrical distribution system somewhere on the sprawling base. He was able to trace the disturbance to Building

138

Eight, the working and sleeping quarters of most of the personnel of the meteorological section, and he telephoned the aerographer on night duty in the building but received no reply. Then he called the section chief, Oskar Krichak, who had a telephone by his bed, and woke him up. Oskar, speaking very calmly, as was his wont, confirmed that the electric light in his room was out; after a brief delay he said, again very calmly, that he smelled smoke. Something was burning, and he would investigate and come right back. Then the phone went dead. The engineer at the power station quickly called his supervisor, Yagodkin, who rushed out in the howling darkness toward Building Eight, accompanied by geological section chief Solovyev.

Yagodkin and Solovyev fought their way over mountainous snow drifts through 120 MPH gusts of wind to the meteorology building, which was on the outskirts of the base. Its roof was covered by a layer of snow six feet thick, but flames were coming out of the personnel hatch and through ominous cracks in the snow. Dense clouds of smoke were billowing from the balloon release tower, which was connected to the main building by a 120-foot tunnel. None of the residents could be seen. Unable to enter the under-snow complex, the two men stumbled back and turned in the general fire alarm at the nearest building.

The whole base quickly turned out to fight the blaze with tractors, fire extinguishers, shovels, and anything else that was available. The hastily organized fire brigades tried to pour snow and water on the flames, but the ferocious wind, which knocked men off their feet and kept the inferno under forced draft, made the task insurmountable, and the fire remained out of control for hours. When I first arrived and was handed a shovel, I assumed that the inhabitants of the building had made their escape, and I wondered that none of them were to be seen in the crowd that was fighting the fire. I rushed up to a frantically shoveling friend and asked, "Where are Krichak and the others?"

He looked at me grimly and simply pointed downwards. It took a moment for me to grasp the enormity of it.

"All of them?"

"Yes, all."

By noon the wind and fire had subsided enough for us to start searching for the bodies of the victims. I volunteered for this grim task along with a few other members of the airborne unit. It took us several days of digging and sifting through the ash-strewn snow, charred, fallen timbers, and wind-scattered debris before we could find all the remains and remove them. The men never had a chance. We found Oskar lying on his back in front of what had once been a heavy wooden door separating his private room from the main hall of the house. Apparently he had been overcome by a blast of flame as soon as he had opened the door to investigate, only a few seconds after putting down the phone. Probably by that time it had already been too late to save any of the occupants. Olldrich Kostka and several of the others had enough time to crawl under their bunks, but they had suffocated there. The last man to be found was the tall, powerfully built Igor Popov, who had dashed through the flames to reach the tunnel that led to the balloon release tower. His terribly burned body was found seventy-five feet down the tunnel. Because of the almost total destruction, the cause of the fire was never determined. The electrical breakdown was probably an effect, rather than the cause, but the sequence of events in Building Eight that Wednesday morning is still a mystery.

Besides Oskar Krichak, five other Russian meteorologists and aerologists had been in Building Eight: Anatoli Belolikov, Vasili Samushkov, Alexander Smirnov, Alexei Dergach, and Igor Popov. Kostka of Czechoslovakia and Hans-Christian Popp of the German Democratic Republic also lost their lives. All were exemplary men, possessed of that special spirit of comradeship and self-denial that makes an expedition really work.

Doctor Skeib was at Druzhba Weather Station on the West Ice Shelf at the time, and he was not told the fate of his compatriot until he returned to Mirnyy. Ironically, his return had been delayed by the same blizzard that lashed the base that tragic morning. Had he arrived on schedule, he would have relieved Popp and been in the meteorology building in his place at the time of the fire. Although word of the disaster soon spread around the Antarctic, no information was given out officially until the next of kin were notified.

It was decided that our comrades would be buried in Antarctica. In part, I think that this was because of the adverse psychological effect such a cargo would have on us on the long voyage back. A simple, impressive funeral service was held on August 24, and the entire company of the base marched behind the slowly moving sledge bearing the bodies to our cemetery on a small island north of Mirnyy. Messages of condolence came in from all over the world. A monument was later erected at the grave site, but a more fitting memorial to the explorers was established by giving the names of the deceased to geographical features in Antarctica: mountains, glaciers, and capes.

The base remained in an official state of mourning and an emotional state of shock for a long time. The flag was flown at half-staff, there were no more boisterous parties, no jazz or any other cheerful music was played over the P.A. system for a while. The meteorological program had to be continued to the best of the expedition's ability, of course, and the few surviving members of the section were assisted by volunteers from other disciplines.

I felt the loss of Oskar Krichak especially deeply. Music was our first common ground, and Oskar showed the most intense interest, both critical and emotional, in my jazz records. Indeed, I don't think he would have objected to having jazz played, New Orleans style, at his funeral. The *Oklahoma* album that he had received from Gordon Cartwright inspired him with the thought of composing a similar musical about a Russian rural community, perhaps working in some of his hilarious adventures on a manned weather balloon flight that he once made across southern Russia and the Ukraine, to the amazement of the farming folk along the way. It would have been a marvelous contribution to musical comedy.

Oskar was deeply moved by the early blues pieces. He had some trouble understanding the words that Bessie Smith was singing, but that great voice cut across years and borders and languages to reach his warm and open heart. Even in the scratchy rerecordings from the good old days of Dixieland, he could detect and appreciate the beautiful tones of Bix Beiderbecke and the virtuosity of Louis Armstrong.

Our relationship went far beyond shared tastes in music. Oskar was very frank and open in the many conversations that we had, and I learned a great deal about many subjects from this wise and liberal man. He was fundamentally an optimistic person—indeed, a joyful one. Large in stature and girth, with a thick black moustache and twinkling eyes, Oskar had a jovial appearance that did not deceive, and he was always bubbling with puns and jokes. In fact, he was one of the few people I have ever known who was witty enough to make the same pun funny in two languages. He had an excellent, if quaint, command of English. But he was very serious about his music and his science. Oskar was extremely generous, especially with those most precious gifts, his knowledge and his time. He was always willing to help out with any of my problems, describing the ins and outs of the system, interceding for me whenever necessary, facilitating my projects in any way he could. I think his basic motives were very simple. He sincerely liked and enjoyed people, he drew no distinctions of nationality, and he very deeply desired peace for his country and the world.

9

To the "Pole of Cold"

What extraordinary uncertainties this work exhibits!
Everyday some new fact comes to life—some new obstacle
which threatens the gravest obstruction. I suppose this is
the reason which makes the game so well worth playing.
—*Robert Falcon Scott*

The definite go-ahead signal for the 1960–61 summer traverse into the heart of the Antarctic continent came in midwinter. It had been eagerly anticipated by the men of the glaciology section, which would be responsible for most of the scientific program, and I was especially gratified at being included (though one of my friends cracked that this was mainly because they just wanted to get an agitator like me off the base). Our precise route was not yet determined, but however we went, the traverse would begin at Mirnyy and take us to Vostok Station at the south geomagnetic pole, the coldest place in the world. The planning, preparation, and execution of this elaborate project occupied most of our time and energies for the remainder of the year.

During the early stages of traverse planning, several possible routes were considered. Two major objectives had priority in making the final choice: for scientific purposes the field party should cover a pre-

viously unexplored part of East Antarctica, but it also had the logistical task of delivering fuel and other supplies to Vostok for the following year's work at that lonely outpost. By late winter a preliminary
itinerary had been outlined. The traverse party would follow the existing trail through the crevassed and stormy coastal region to the
vicinity of the abandoned Pionerskaya Station, and then make a new
advance into the interior across the previously unsurveyed area to the
west of the old trail to Vostok. From a *Tochka Povorota* (turning
point) in this virgin territory, we would then return to the old trail at
Komsomolskaya, reopen that ministation for the summer, and then
drive directly over the top of the polar plateau to Vostok. Our return
from Vostok was still up in the air. We might then drive back overland by another route if we had the time, or else be flown back to
Mirnyy. This could not be decided until relatively late in the season.
Scientifically, this plan promised to add another dimension to the still
sketchy picture of a vast sector of the hinterland, which so far was
known in depth only from the previous traverses along the profile
from Mirnyy to Vostok and the south pole, and the spur from Komsomolskaya to Sovietskaya.

There was plenty of strenuous argument, and even some table-
pounding, during the planning process. After all, it involved the integration of the desires and requirements of several strongly interested
and highly opinionated groups—to say nothing of some hard-nosed
individuals. The glaciologists and geophysicists wanted the broadest
possible coverage of the ice sheet and the underlying bedrock for their
scientific observations. The transport section, which had the burden
of providing the vehicles and driver-mechanics from a limited motor
pool, had as its primary goal the resupply of Vostok. Polyarnaya
Aviatsiya would be risking its crews and craft making airdrops of fuel
deep in the interior of the continent, and it would be on call around
the clock for emergency and possibly search and rescue operations.
The expedition leadership had to reconcile our operations in the field
with those at Mirnyy, Vostok, and Lazarev, and the arrival of the
ships with the new expedition in the summer. Agreements were finally hammered out after prolonged sessions in the Pentagon. I was getting practical experience in how the dual system of party-state administration could go out of sync and produce bureaucratic chaos.

The target date for the beginning of the traverse was tentatively set for the end of October, the middle of spring astronomically, but still a pretty wintry time in the Antarctic. In the interim, the glaciology-geophysics group was kept busy in the coastal region. We completed the glaciological polygon in the crevasse *dzhungli* (jungle), as we called it, during September, despite the bitter trials of violent *purga* weather that inflicted numerous cases of frostbite on our faces and hands. Later that month and in the early part of October we returned to the ice shelves to continue the glaciological, seismic, and gravimetric measurements that had been begun in March and April, and we also flew out across the still-frozen Davis Sea to investigate the immense, mysterious Pobeda ice island.

Our work on the ice shelves and the huge ice island was in the nature of a dress rehearsal for the inland traverse. We were doing much the same kind of work, except that in the coastal region we operated from a *samolet* (airplane), whereas on the over-snow traverse we would be traveling in a *sanno-traktornyy poyezd* (sled-tractor train). Once again, we were based in a central tent camp on the Zapadnyy Shelfovyy Lednik (West Ice Shelf), from which the field party fanned out to survey points.

This time we had a lot more room and more convenient facilities. We also ate a lot better than before, and each of us took a turn at the cooking. An old-timer who came out to visit remarked on the excellent *kolbasa* (sausage) that we were enjoying: "Here I am in this god-forsaken place, eating much better than I did in my youth. In those days you never saw meat this good. In that time either the speculators hoarded it, or the state requisitioned it."

When the *burya* closed in, I once again heard the tales told by the snowbound. They were often as touching and bizarre as those of Mikhail Lermontov or Anton Chekhov. Now I was better able to understand the nuances than I had been half a year before. Stories could be about the riotous Gypsy wedding that was supposed to settle a feud between two clans, but failed and ended with the stabbing death of the bridegroom; the beautiful young woman who had to reject her lover and marry a wealthy old man for the sake of her family; the prominent party official who surreptitiously had his child baptized to humor an influential aunt; the compulsive gambler in the wild and lawless Soviet Far East who had lost everything at the tables, finally wagered his wife, and lost her, too. The poignant stories of modern—and eternal—Russia went on and on against the background of howling, shrieking wind, punctuated by the snaps and jerks of the tent frame.

On this trip I acquired a new name. My friends had trouble pronouncing "Gus," which my family and friends at home call me—it came out sounding like "Guess." But now Pavel Kutuzov found a Slavic nickname for me. We had brought the husky pup Pulya with us as a pet, feeling that the roly-poly creature's adult life of sledging work would begin soon enough, and she decided to adopt me as a foster parent. After I crawled into my dog-pelt sleeping bag at night, Pulya would climb on top of it and curl up, gradually inching closer and closer to the small opening that I left near my face for breathing. Sometimes she would perch right over my head, a fact of which I would be only semiconsciously aware. Then I would "erupt," and Pulya would scamper to the other end of the tent, to creep back and start her encroachment again. My indulgent treatment of our canine camp-follower led Pavel to call me "Dyadya Gil" (Uncle Gil), and "Dyadya" I thenceforth became.

From the West Ice Shelf we flew to the Shackleton Shelf, where we were able to accomplish rather more in the way of ice-thickness measurements and snow studies than we had on our abortive visits in the fall. We tackled the problem of nearby Pobeda—was this nine-hundred-square-mile slab of ice a section of the ice shelf that had separated from the rest but was still firmly grounded and maintaining itself against ablation, or was it just an enormous tabular iceberg that had temporarily run aground? In the short time that we had to investigate, our group found that while Pobeda was largely afloat, it was wedge-shaped in cross-section and securely anchored at two points along its thicker side. Most probably it was a remnant of a much more extensive ice shelf from Antarctica's more heavily glaciated past. The prognosis for its survival was not very favorable.

We returned to Mirnyy in mid-October (the equivalent of April in the northern hemisphere) to complete our preparations for the over-snow traverse. The three ATT tractors that we were going to use for transport required considerable *remont* (overhaul or repair). The ATT (pronounced "ah-tay-tay") was a World War II model artillery tractor of heavy-gauge steel construction and weighed more than twenty-seven tons. This *tyagach* (tractor, or prime mover) was powered by a five-hundred-horsepower V-12 diesel engine of a highly successful design that had been used in several different types of Soviet heavy vehicles. The transmission had five forward speeds. In second gear, which was normal for a snow surface, it made a speed of about five kilometers per hour (three MPH) under a full load. The original half-meter wide tracks had been replaced by special snow tracks that were three-quarters of a meter wide because in soft snow the standard size tracks would simply chew down until the mechanical monster lay immobilized on its undercarriage, spinning its tracks helplessly. The Russian word for a tractor's crawler track is *gusenitsa* (literally, "caterpillar"), and, as in the United States, the term is used loosely to refer to the whole tractor. Puns are seldom translatable, and I heard no equivalent for the American expression "cat-skinner."

On two of these powerful vehicles were mounted little houses (what we would call a wanigan, and the Russians *balok*. These would be our living quarters for the duration of the traverse. The three sledges we would be hauling, which measured eight by three meters, were fitted with heavy frames of steel L-beams so that three tiers of fuel barrels could be securely loaded on each. The drilling rig for our seismic shooting (hand-drilling would no longer be adequate for the deep shot-holes needed in the soft snow of the interior) was mounted at the rear of one sledge, and sheds were built at the rear of the other two, one for a glaciological cold laboratory and the other for general storage. Fortunately, we were aided in the extensive outdoor construction work needed to put all this together by volunteers from all over the base.

The science *balok* contained the seismic recording apparatus, a small darkroom, two upper and two lower bunks, a gas cooking stove, a small oil stove for heating, water tanks, and fire extinguishers. Most of the remaining space would be taken up by food stores and personal gear. An intercom connected the *balok* with the tractor cab, where the driver had a mobile radio set for communication with the other *balok*, which contained our long-distance radio station and the navigation equipment. This other *balok*, called the "flag *balok*," or command center, had two broad shelves for sleeping eight men and a plastic bubble in the roof for navigational observations. The third tractor carried no *balok*, but it was loaded with repair gear and spare parts for all the tractors in its aft cargo bay. In the event of radio failure signal flares could be used for communication between vehicles.

The leader of the traverse was the expedition's transport section chief, an energetic and somewhat bombastic man named Boris Krasnikov. He chose as driver-mechanics Ivan Bubel, a mechanical wizard, Yuri Birger, a veteran *polyarnik* and onetime Moscow cab driver, and young Viktor Kantuev. Geodesist Vladimir Maltsev would do the navigating, the younger Boris Kazadaev would serve as our radioman, and Inokhenty Shastin, the younger of the two physicians at Mirnyy, would handle our medical problems and double as chef. Unlike Barashkov, the military surgeon, Shastin had been too young for World War II, but he had treated children who were napalmed in Korea, and was a fervent pacifist. Vyacheslav Ivanov, head of the glaciology section, was the scientific leader and would perform the glaciological and meteorological observations. Vitaly Tsukernik, Vladimir Maksakov, and I would carry out seismic shooting and other geophysical measurements, except for magnetometer readings by Maltsev, and Boris Zakhariev was the drilling engineer. Krasnikov, Bubel, Birger, Kantuev, and Maltsev had already been trailhardened by working on the tractor train that had delivered fuel and supplies to the Komsomolskaya substation from late February to early April.

Shortly after our return from airborne operations we began loading the *sani* (sledges) with fuel barrels. The depot was now covered with a hard crust of wind-toughened snow, and it was like pulling teeth with crowbars and a small mobile crane to get the drums extracted. In all we stacked 302 barrels on the sturdy sledges; the total net weight of fuel came to about seventy-five metric tons. Under these heavy loads—*baloks*, sledges, fuel drums, equipment, supplies—the fuel consumption of each ATT diesel was expected to be a whopping seven or eight liters per kilometer (or about three gallons per mile). At this estimated rate of oil consumption we would use up about half our cargo on the projected sixteen-hundred-kilometer trip to Vostok. Since the station needed forty tons of fuel for the winter, we would have to receive airdrops of fuel en route to make up the deficit.

To help nourish the inner man, Venediktov organized a "*pelmeni* party" for us. *Pelmeni*, a Siberian specialty, consists of ground meat, onion, pepper, and garlic rolled in dumplings of dough somewhat like wonton. These treats were prepared in the *kayut kompaniya* by a large company of worker-revelers who merrily combined food making and festivities like dancing and singing. The atmosphere was like an old-fashioned American cooking bee or barn-raising. The vast quantity of *pelmeni* produced was frozen and stored for the traverse, when the bite-sized morsels would be boiled with butter to provide quick, tasty meals. The rest of the food for the journey was collected by the traverse personnel and the station cooks from the capacious under-snow storerooms that branched off behind the *kayut kompaniya*. The fare included beefsteaks, hamburger, mutton, chicken, beef tongue, canned pork tongue, sausage, herring, canned crabmeat ("export quality"), potatoes, beans, boiled eggs, fruit compote, black bread, hardtack, fruitcake, and a giant wheel of cheese. We took a large supply of black tea and, for condiments, garlic, peppers, tomato sauce, jam, and the inevitable chopped eggplant.

The preparations were now well under way, and the departure date was advanced to October 24. Tsukernik and Zakhariev had some further work to do around Mirnyy, so they planned to fly out and join us a few days later, before we broke away from the old trail to Pionerskaya and began our scientific investigations in earnest. At that time, Korotkevich and Venediktov would also come out for a final conference with us about the traverse route, our itinerary, and last-minute operational details.

Antarctica is conventionally divided into two parts, East Antarctica, the bulkier sector that lies mostly, but not precisely, within the eastern hemisphere, and West Antarctica, the smaller, irregularly shaped part that faces the southern Atlantic and Pacific Oceans. These regions are quite different geologically. East Antarctica is largely a stable continental platform of very old rocks that have been little disturbed for hundreds of millions of years. West Antarctica consists of more recently formed and distorted rocks and still-active structures, including the southern continuation of the Andes, and much of its underlying crust is not as thick and fully continental as that of East Antarctica.

East Antarctica is now perceived, according to the new tectonics of modern geology, as formerly part of the primordial southern supercontinent, Gondwanaland. This protocontinent split into several pieces that have been separating for the last 150 million years. The other continental fragments—southern Africa, Madagascar, southern India, Australia, and part of South America—also contain stable "shield" areas like East Antarctica. The separation occurred, and is still occurring, along what are now suboceanic ridges, like the one our ship crossed on the voyage through the Indian Ocean. I should mention that this was a minority view of the world in 1960, although geology was going through profound changes.

Both sectors of Antarctica are mostly covered by a permanent layer of ice several thousand feet thick, but the East Antarctic lobe of the giant continental ice sheet is much larger and higher and, some researchers think, more stable than the West Antarctic ice. Antarctica's present ice cover is thought to be a few million years old, and glaciers expanded and contracted across its surface in the more distant past. Evidence of glaciation in the early Permian period (about 280 million years ago) in Antarctica and such widely separated places as South America, South Africa, Australia, and India helped convince many geologists that these land masses were once parts of a supercontinental whole. Southern hemisphere geologists, and especially those who have worked in the Antarctic, were among the first to be won over to the new, dynamic ideas about the history of the earth's crust. The rather conservative Russian school has tended to resist these concepts, which is interesting in view of their markedly "dialectical" nature. The new theory involves continuous processes of interconnected motion and opposition and both evolutionary and revolutionary episodes of geological transformation.

Direct measurement of the thickness of the Antarctic ice sheet was a fairly recent development. The first real geophysical traverse that used seismic sounding in a systematic way to investigate the ice along a profile into the interior was carried out by the Norwegian-British-Swedish expedition of 1949–52. The methods used in this pioneering venture were refined in Greenland, which has the world's second largest ice sheet, and applied on an extensive scale in Antarctica during the IGY. The great era of the over-snow traverses, criss-crossing and probing the continent to measure the ice and outline the subglacial topography, lasted for about a decade and a half after the IGY. In 1960 it was in full swing, with Soviet, American, and Japanese tractor parties piercing the frozen ramparts to wrest secrets from the white continent.

The big day ("D-Day," as my companions called it) arrived with bright sunshine and warm zephyrs to match our buoyant spirits. We left early in the morning, after a formal farewell ceremony that included a round of champagne toasts at a little table set up in the snow at the head of the trail. The whole base turned out to see us off, and many of our friends followed us for miles, snapping photos of the tractor train with their Russian- and East German-made cameras and shouting wishes for good luck through the roar of the diesels. Then we began chugging up the meandering road through the familiar crevasse field, and the last of our well-wishers fell away. Our little band was now alone in the awesome immensity of the Antarctic interior, on a journey that would last for several months and take us across one of the few remaining empty spaces on the surface of the globe.

The first 135 kilometers of the traverse took three days to cover. The heavy tractors had to wind their way slowly up the grade and around the giant crevasses at the edge of the continental glacier, following sporadic barrel and flag markers that were often nearly invisible in the fiercely blowing snow. The beautiful weather that had favored our departure lasted barely long enough to see us out of Mirnyy. At this time of year, the wind flowed steadily down the slopes of the ice sheet and kept the loose snow constantly suspended in the air. The engines labored ominously, and the fuel consumption of each tractor shot up to an alarming fourteen liters per kilometer (six gallons per mile).

Maltsev (or "Prince Vladimir the Navigator," as he was dubbed) was soon bedeviled by a navigational problem that persisted until we got out of this stormy zone at the margin of the plateau: the tractors couldn't travel close together because the compass in the flag *balok* was compensated only for the deviation caused by its (and its sledge's) own magnetic effect, and the massive concentration of steel in another tractor-sledge combination nearby would throw it wildly off and make our heading utterly unreliable. On the other hand, we couldn't separate the vehicles by very much, or we would lose sight of one another in the driving snow, and the other two ATT's would get lost. Sometimes visibility became so bad that we simply had to "circle the wagons," shut down, and wait for the stormgods of the Antarctic to relax their icy grip.

On this leg of the journey Vyacheslav Ivanov and I made a set of glaciological and gravimetric observations at several points, and I also helped Ivanov obtain a photographic record of the apparently monotonous landscape, which on closer inspection had a surprisingly intricate texture. He had already compiled a classification of *sastrugi*, or wind-formed features of the snow surface, in the Soviet Arctic, and he was interested in seeing how their Antarctic counterparts fitted into his scheme. Ivanov also made meteorological observations every six hours, and these data were immediately radioed back to Mirnyy by Kazadaev for incorporation into the synoptic weather forecasts.

I found that the traverse conditions posed a few problems for my gravity measurements. It was impractical to shut the engines down at every stop, but the motor's vibrations made the delicate gravimeter unreadable, so I had to put a good distance between myself and the ATT's before taking a reading. Even when the engines were killed, my ultrasensitive instrument was perturbed by the ground roll set up by the *baloks* and sledges shaking in the wind. During our operations on the frigid glaciological polygon I had come up with a way to keep the gravimeter batteries warm enough to work properly. I wore them close to my (presumably warm) body and connected them to the meter by an extension cord that led out through my heavy clothes. The brightness of the sun at midday, often diffused by whiteout conditions, was so intense that I had to make a protective hood that would fall over the instrument and allow my eyes to distinguish the calibration marks in the dimly lit eyepiece.

The science *balok* was not a very comfortable home. What with the pervasive roar of the engine, the constant mechanical vibrations, and the nauseating odor of diesel exhaust, I was reminded of my first polar experience on the American icebreaker *Northwind*, except that the Coast Guard vessel had jolted up and down only when crunching the ice floes, not every few seconds, as our tractor did. Even staying warm was not easy, as we had continual difficulties with the temperamental oil feeder and the draft of the smokestack on the space heater. The stack had a nasty propensity to back up and fill the *balok* with black, oily fumes.

At meal times the whole traverse party crowded into our *balok*, but while we were running only Shastin, Ivanov, and Volodya (short for Vladimir) Maksakov shared the boxcarlike lodgings with me. Naturally we engaged in interminable conversations, completely in

Russian now, for nobody else in the party (except Vitaly, who had not yet joined us) knew more than a smattering of English, and I was beginning to think that I had forgotten it. Food cases and a couple of *samosval* (literally, self-collapsing) camp stools were our seats. The flimsy *samosvaly* were one of the "standing" jokes of the trip, for they did, indeed, collapse themselves, seemingly of their own volition, at unexpected moments. We also had a folding card table whose structural intricacies only Volodya Maksakov had mastered, and even Volodya needed a strong partner to help set it up.

Sometimes I rode in the flag *balok* and talked tractors, navigation, and radio with Krasnikov, Maltsev, and Kazadaev. The transceiver that the latter operated was a military model, and it bore the stenciled cautionary legend: "Be careful—the enemy is listening!" But somebody had crossed out the word *vrag* (enemy) and written in *drug* (friend).

On October 27 we stopped at kilometer 135 of the old trail and waited for the airplane to fly out from Mirnyy. Despite the foul weather, we had surmounted the steep and jagged glacis of Fortress Antarctica without mishap and were now well up on the ice plateau, at an altitude of 1,680 meters (5,500 feet). We knew from previous investigations that bedrock was right about at sea level, so there was a good mile of solid ice beneath our tracks. Maltsev did an astronomical fix and confirmed that our coordinates were 67° 44′ south, 93° 46′ east. Our latitude was the same, in the Northern Hemisphere, as that of Lapland or the northern part of the Trans-Alaska Pipeline. It was naturally considerably colder at this height than at Mirnyy. The temperature had dropped from +10° F when we left the station to −35° F, and it was still very windy, so the chill really bit.

An LI-2 piloted by aviation chief Aleksander Pimenov came in right on schedule for the field rendezvous and made a perfect ski landing on the rough snow and ice surface. After we had helped Vitaly and Boris unload their gear and stow it in the *baloks* we all gathered for the final conference with Korotkevich, Venediktov, and Pimenov. The main topic was time, which would be the crucial factor from now on.

It was decided that we would break away from the old trail at our present position (about 235 kilometers short of Pionerskaya) and strike out to the southwest into unknown territory until we reached another turning point, which we arbitrarily fixed at 72° south, 87° east. From there we would head back to the southeast and drive directly toward the mothballed Komsomolskaya substation, completing two sides of a triangle of which the third was the old trail.

Upon arrival at Komsomolskaya it would be our responsibility not only to put the outpost into operation as a weather, communications, and safety facility for flights between Mirnyy and Vostok, but also to man it until we could be relieved by the incoming personnel of the Sixth Expedition. From Komsomolskaya the traverse party, reduced in manpower and, unfortunately, scientific program, would follow the old trail to Vostok to deliver our cargo of fuel and supplies. Whether we would have time for any kind of return traverse from Vostok was problematical at this point. That was it. We shook hands all around, bid our visitors goodbye, and watched their plane whip up a snowcloud as it took off and climbed back to the north. We were on our own.

The bad weather of the first few days followed us on our new heading, and after making only sixty-five kilometers in forty-eight hours we halted in the face of violent snow-laden winds that reduced our visibility to the length of a single tractor-sledge combination. There we sat for two days, as we had on the ice shelves. Huddled around the stove, drinking heavily buttered tea, and constantly talking, we were inaccessible to the outside world except through Kazadaev's shortwave radio. We had healthy appetites and wolfed down large quantities of the mutton, hamburger, boiled potatoes, baked beans, and thick beef soup that Shastin dished out. And despite the swaying of the rigs in the wind, we all slept very soundly.

I found it immensely satisfying to burrow into a warm sleeping bag, while only a few inches above my head, outside the shelter, a frigid, snow-heavy current of air roared by that could have frozen the life out of me in a shockingly short time if I was exposed to it. It seemed like having a joke on death, and the impression was all the more enhanced by knowing that everywhere around, in some directions for thousands of miles, everything on the planet was utterly cold and virtually lifeless.

When that bitter wind finally dropped, and the sky cleared to an oceanic blue, we all grabbed shovels and tackled the enormous snowdrifts that by this time had nearly submerged all three tractor trains.

The ATTs were warmed up and checked out, everything lying around loose was secured, and we resumed our back-jarring odyssey into the white void.

We were now really there, deep in the frozen heartland of the earth's greatest wilderness. There was not a single trace of man's "mastery" of the world in the millions of square miles that lay around us, except perhaps some air pollution that circulated even there. The polar plateau is a simple world, and its beauty lies in its austerity. It has no hills or valleys, no trees, no boulders. There is nothing but that endless glistening whiteness, broken only by an occasional wind ripple in the snow and matched above by the completely cloudless blue sky. Except for the yearly alternation of polar day and night, the inland ice is unchanging in time as well as space. In other places it gets almost as cold as in the interior of Antarctica, as in the *taiga* (coniferous forest) of eastern Siberia, but there the dreadful cold is only in winter, and then the land is only sleeping. In summer the *taiga* awakens to warmth and life, fir trees grow rapidly, wildflowers blossom, the lynx and wolf pursue their scurrying prey through damp woodlands and green meadows, and swarms of gnats and mosquitoes fill the air. But in summer the polar plateau is as barren as it is in winter, and the "white desert" is just not quite so cold. With the summer sun slanting its weak rays across the still-frozen snowscape, death changes the color of its shrouds from black to white, but it is no less dead.

This was one of the few periods during the expedition when we had time to do very much meditating. As we slowly rode over the endless plateau our minds were for once liberated from the usual bonds of immediate action and response. I could sit there in the tractor cab or the *balok* and ponder the long trail that had brought me here to the broad back of this vast, cold, white country, which all of us had sought so avidly and which now surrounded us so ominously. But was it the wasteland that we really sought, or was it the integrating effect that this menacing environment had upon the social consciousness of our little community? Was it perhaps the fellowship of the human band, tribally strengthened by the tempering pressures of the wilderness around us? Was it a revolt against the atomism, the alienation of the ordinary "civilized" life so characteristic of both our countries? Had we really been seeking the heightened sense of humanity that grows from a communal struggle against hardship and peril? It is paradoxical that we must leave most of our species behind to revalidate our membership in it.

I thought about my companions, these stolid-looking men of the east, so seemingly different in their background, their heritage, their daily lives, and yet so uncannily similar in their sensibilities and aspirations. Nikolai Gogol, in a famous passage, wrote of Russia as a great troika, or three-horse sleigh, hurtling madly across the world. Our vehicles were not exactly hurtling, and they lacked the grace of the horse-drawn sleigh, but they were certainly rolling inexorably across our grim part of the world. And to me that great enigma, Russia, was symbolized just as well, perhaps even better, by our unglamorous ATT tractors and their overloaded sledges, ponderous and ungainly, but nevertheless moving on, and somehow, inevitable. But the question still remains, to where?

We rumbled on over the snow, passing through a region of relatively large *sastrugi*, as much as eighty centimeters high. These unusual features were of great interest, even excitement, to Ivanov, but they made for even less comfortable travel than before, and they worried the drivers as the ancient tractors banged and rattled their way across the washboard surface. It was not standard operating procedure for them to change course and seek an easier route, since it was not worth the time and fuel that a zigzag path through the obstacles would entail. I found this out when I took over the controls of one of the tractors for a while and started to veer away from a shadowy mound. Yuri thumped me vigorously on the shoulder and shouted in my ear, "Nyet, nyet, pryamoi dorogoi!" (No, no, straight ahead!)

On November 3 we reached kilometer 265 from Mirnyy and spent the whole day on our first complex scientific station. Glaciological, gravimetric, and magnetic observations were made, as they had been at shorter intervals along the route, but the biggest job was seismic depth-sounding. Boris Zakhariev cranked up his power auger and drilled down thirty meters into the snow and firn to provide the seismologists with an energy-efficient shot-hole. Temperature measurements were first taken in the bore-hole for glaciological and climatological studies, and then Boris and Vitaly loaded it with explosives and tamped it with snow for the first shot. Meanwhile, Volodya and I laid out the seismic cable and planted and attached the geophones to pick up the echoes of the blast from beneath the surface. On an American doodlebugging crew, this function is performed by a "jug hustler" (a "jug" being a geophone), and I believe that I deserve the credit, or criticism, for introducing this Texas terminology into the Russian language. Vitaly checked out the filters and amplifiers and the tape- and photo-recording system, and when everything was in order we yelled, "Tishe!"

Everyone froze, and Vitaly then called on the phone from the instrument panel in the science *balok* to Boris at the shot point, "Pregotovitsya . . . Vzryv!"

Boris set off the blasting machine, and the dull thump of the explosion was felt, rather than heard. A geyser of fine snow came out of the shot-hole. Several more shots were made (a "sprung hole" that has already been fired is more efficient in transmitting seismic energy than a new one), and we did a preliminary analysis of the seismogram data. At this location, which Maltsev established as 68° 47′ south, 96° 21′ east, the echoes from the ice-rock interface at the bottom of the glacier indicated an ice thickness of 1,970 meters (6,500 feet). Our elevation, estimated from barometric observations, was 2,180 meters (7,200 feet), so the actual surface of the continent, underneath all that ice, was only about 210 meters (700 feet) above sea level.

Dr. Shastin's medical practice had been practically nonexistent so far, especially since the "finger doctor," as I was inelegantly called, had brought along an abundant supply of Band-aids and Mercurochrome. But suddenly the usually cheerful and carefree Volodya began to be moody and cranky, and then complained of abdominal pains. Shastin examined him and made a tentative diagnosis of appendicitis. He was taking no chances, and had Kazadaev radio for an airplane to fly the surgeon, Dr. Barashkov, out from Mirnyy for a second opinion. The little AN-2 was promptly dispatched, but it developed engine trouble and had to return to base. Shortly afterward an LI-2, manned by our old friends from the ice-shelf surveys, Sasha and Fedya, made the flight successfully, and the surgeon took Volodya back with him for observation. The very next day we were informed that his appendix had been removed and his condition was excellent, but he would not be able to rejoin the field party before we reached Komsomolskaya.

On the same day as Volodya Maksakov's operation one of the tractors came down with its own ailment. It burned out a couple of crank-shaft bearings. This was a severe blow to the traverse because it meant a delay of two days while we pulled out the engine block and replaced the bearings. We began this exercise by drawing up a sledge on each side of the damaged engine and laying a stout log, which had been brought along for just this sort of problem, between the sledges. A heavy-duty chain hoist was suspended from the log and used to raise the engine. Unfortunately, the ATT had not been designed for ease of repair, and the pulling and hauling, uncoupling and detaching seemed interminable. We worked around the clock on this job, each man going inside only for a few winks of sleep and some hot food. The temperature was −34° F, and the wind speed about twenty knots, and I remarked on the stoicism of my companions in the face of these high wind-chill conditions to Ivanov. He nodded, "Yes, that quality of ours had a lot to do with winning the war. When the weather was like this at the front, the enemy stayed in their bunkers drinking schnapps, but we stayed out there in the cold, repairing our tanks." Then he laughed and added, prophetically, "This is sort of like a war here, and the Antarctic is using Russian strategy on us—drawing us into its vast interior and gradually wearing us down."

The geophysicists made good use of the down time to carry out a seismic sounding at this point. With the departure of Volodya we had to rearrange the division of labor, and I had been promoted to the task of giving the check-out and firing orders over the field telephone. The first time I did this, I used my best command voice—but alas, I had already told my companions about my brief military career, in which I had reached the exalted rank of corporal. When my imperious voice came booming over the wires, somebody interjected, in mock awe, "Govorit kaporal!" (The corporal speaks!)

It stuck with me. Not only did "The Corporal" become another of my nicknames, but whenever my manner became too didactic someone would always pipe up, "Govorit kaporal!"

The order of march had become routine to us by now. We rose at about 7 A.M. (Mirnyy local time), had a hearty breakfast, and drove for four hours. Then we stopped for a light lunch and inspection of our rigs, and drove again until supper time (7 P.M.). After a full dinner we drove till early morning, when we all turned in for a few hours' sleep, which was nearly impossible while the machines were in motion. A major stop, where we carried out the complete program of seismological, gravity, magnetic, glaciological, geodetic, snow temperature, and meteorological observations, took at least one full day, and sometimes two. Between these seismic stations we made short stops about every fifteen kilometers for gravity, magnetic, glaciological, and meteorological measurements.

One evening, while I was riding in the cab with Yuri and Boris, talking tractors and heavy equipment—names like Case, Joy, Allis-Chalmers, Euclid, Caterpillar, and Bucyrus-Erie are household words among Soviet engineers—Boris, with his usual straight face, suddenly pulled a map of Antarctica out of one of his capacious pockets with a flourish. He peered at it intently, and, like a Sunday motorist consulting his auto club road map, said, "Well, where would you fellows like to go today?" It was a nice thought, but everything looked the same, and anyway we were already committed to a great circle course.

We jokingly opted for the slow, scenic route. We were still climbing the slopes of the ice plateau, but the ascent had now become so gradual that the surface around us appeared to be completely flat, and it all looked like one big road. Looking across that seemingly endless expanse of white snow, featureless except for furrows of low *sastrugi* like frozen waves, I was reminded of Melville's hero Ishmael and the advice he received from the old ship's captain when he said that he wanted to see the world: look out over the harbor—water like that is about all you'll see of the world on a whaling expedition. Similarly, white snow and more snow is pretty much all you'll see of the world on a journey across central Antarctica.

A serious magnetic disturbance associated with spectacular auroral displays in the Northern Hemisphere (it was too light now in the Antarctic for us to see the southern lights) blacked out our radio communication with Mirnyy for several days, but we still heard the nightly news from Radio Moscow, and on November 13 the ether cleared enough for me to receive my first message from home since we had left the base. It was relayed by an old amateur radio friend, "Doc" Haus, who had been an unseen but very important electronic presence at Wilkes Station, and who had recently visited my family in California. We were very much in his debt, for just after the Mirnyy fire, when rumors and garbled accounts of the disaster were being leaked abroad, he had notified my parents that I was safe—just in time, before a misinformed reporter called them for some obituary background on their late son.

On November 16 we had our first airdrop of fuel: an IL-12 twin-engine cargo plane buzzed the traverse party and released five barrels, one at a time, in free fall. It was a spectacular scene, with the aircraft flying over us at a hundred feet off the ground, and each drum hitting the surface in a tremendous plume of snow, then bouncing erratically end over end until it came to an abrupt halt about a hundred yards from the point of impact. Remarkably, all the barrels landed intact. On the harder surface near the coast, the breakage rate of air-dropped barrels was quite high, but the snow up here on the plateau was soft enough to cushion the shock. Polyarnaya Aviatsiya delivered most of our remaining en-route fuel requirements in several more dramatic drops over the next few days. We stacked the new drums on the sledges—another laborious operation—to replace the drained barrels that had been left along our track as markers.

As the traverse party approached the outer *Tochka Povorota*, the weather was generally clear and calm, though we had occasional gusty winds of up to twenty-five knots, and even a light fall of snow, a rarity in this desertlike region. The temperature was still dropping, though the spring warming tended to counteract the effects of increasing altitude and latitude. The days were getting progressively longer, and for some time the sun had been lazily circling the horizon and barely skimming below it around the chronological midnight. On November 18 there was no sunset at all, and from then until the end of the traverse the sun was continuously above the horizon, making one very long day.

We reached the *Tochka Povorota* on November 23. Maltsev made an especially thorough geodetic fix here that put us at 71° 59′ south, 87° 00′ west. Our most accurate odometer, in the flag tractor, showed that we had come 671 kilometers (420 miles) from Mirnyy in just under a month of toil and travel. We spent two full days on this spot and made a complete set of scientific observations. The seismic shooting turned out to be very difficult here, as the wind had kicked up again and there was a great deal of blowing snow and a high background-noise level, not to mention the usual frostbitten hands and faces. Nevertheless, we obtained some good seismic echoes and determined that the ice sheet here was 2,730 meters (9,000 feet) thick. Our altitude was now 3,100 meters (10,200 feet) above sea level, so we were parked nearly two miles above a subglacial rise that reached at least 370 meters (1,200 feet) above the sea.

Beyond the *Tochka Povorota* we entered a region of extremely soft snow and very low, broad *sastrugi*. Even the extra-wide tracks sank very deeply into the snow, and sometimes a tractor would be stopped dead, churning its *gusenitsi* in place. The only advantage was that now the ride was somewhat more comfortable. But our seismic investigations were hampered because the sides of the bore-holes were prone to collapse, and we had to drill down fifty meters to get thirty meters of usable depth. We even had to use larger amounts of dynamite because so much of the seismic energy was being absorbed by the acoustically resistant snow. A person walking across the surface would produce a domino effect of collapsing snow crust that would ripple out from each step in all directions, and it was very difficult to get conditions quiet enough to take a decent reading with the sensitive gravimeter.

It was getting colder as we moved southward and upward. The temperature was now generally varying betwen −20° and −40° F, and we had an even colder snap near the end of November, when it dropped to −51° F. The sky was cloudless, but it contained tiny, beautifully refracting ice crystals, and the sun was frequently the center of a brilliant display of halos and sun dogs. Oxygen deficiency in the atmosphere was becoming noticeable as we approached the 11,000-foot level, and with moderate exercise we found ourselves laboring to fill our lungs. In Antarctica the stratosphere is lower than it is elsewhere in the world, and with increasing altitude the rarefaction of oxygen is intensified, as is its effect on the human system. During the summer the effective altitude (called the "pressure altitude") here was about 14,000 feet. Since we had been increasing our elevation gradually, we were avoiding the acclimatization problems of those who are transported suddenly to the polar plateau from sea level (the adverse effects are usually felt for about a week), but even slow-moving traverse parties feel appreciable long-term effects.

Another major tractor repair problem arose on the first of December, when one of the transmissions went out. We had to replace it—another two-day job with the logs and chain hoist, long hours contorted into uncomfortable positions within the cold steel of the machinery, and the ever-present hazards of frostbite and hypothermia. When we had finished that operation, we made about thirty more kilometers and then had bearing trouble again, which required another half-day's work. Russians are fairly stoical, but they are by no means a docile or a fatalistic people, and the griping I heard at this juncture was reminiscent of that of the Navy Seabees I used to work with—even to the translation of some of the epithets. The repeated delays because of bad weather and vehicle breakdowns had taken up an inordinate share of the summer season, and we were beginning to wonder just when we would finally limp into Komsomolskaya Station.

As it turned out, limp we did, for two of our party quite literally. Early on the morning of December 7, Maltsev confidently informed us that Komsomolskaya lay dead ahead. It was not yet visible, and we were skeptical of such pinpoint reckoning, but sure enough, before long a little mound of black dots appeared on the horizon—all that could be seen of the nearly snow-covered buildings. We were still a few kilometers from our goal when Yuri Birger's tractor ran out of fuel. The other two drivers were fearful of not being able to start again in the extraordinarily soft snow if they once stopped, so they ground on inexorably toward the station. Yuri and Boris Zakhariev, who was riding shotgun with him, jumped enthusiastically out of the lifeless caterpillar and proceeded on foot to Komsomolskaya; they sank deep into the featherlike snow with every step and were exhausted when they finally reached the station. We uncoupled the sledge from the flag tractor and drove it back to the stalled machine for the refueling. The unburdened ATT threw up great clouds of fine snow as it all but flew over the fluffy surface in the little-used third gear. The metal itself almost seemed to rejoice, like a draft horse unhitched from a heavy wagon and frolicking in a pasture. We refueled by siphoning oil from one tractor tank to the other. I had the honor of this little maneuver, and I can honestly say that there's nothing quite like getting a mouthful of diesel oil at forty below!

We celebrated our arrival and the completion of the primary scientific tasks of the traverse in traditional Russian style, with a round of vodka toasts. The traverse party had come 1,081 kilometers (670 miles), most of it over previously unexplored territory, and had significantly enlarged the picture of subglacial topography in East Antarctica. We made a final seismic shot in the vicinity of Komsomolskaya and found the ice thickness to be 3,370 meters (11,100 feet), while the snow surface elevation was estimated at 3,500 meters (11,500 feet); hence, the bedrock at this point is only about 130 meters (400 feet) above sea level, despite the great distance from the coast. For collectors of geographical oddities, this location, 74° 06′ south, 97° 30′ east, has an interesting distinction: here the "north" end of a compass needle points due west.

In retrospect, the combined seismic, gravimetric, and magnetic observations that we had made along the traverse route indicated that the ice sheet we had been crossing covered a low bedrock plateau indented by several valleys, including one major depression. The subglacial plateau rises to three gentle summits and reaches its maximum elevation about 200 kilometers past our outer turning point, where it is 700 meters (2,300 feet) above sea level. The depression is part of a huge, unexplained depressed zone between the coastal and interior regions of East Antarctica, and our discoveries showed that it extends several hundred kilometers farther west than was previously known. In its trough, just before our turning point, it drops below sea level (if the ice were removed, however, the unburdening of the land would make it rise, a phenomenon called *isostatic rebound*).

We found that the mean thickness of the ice sheet along the whole profile was an impressive 2,400 meters (7,900 feet, or about a mile and a half), and the ice reaches its maximum depth near Komsomolskaya, at 3,600 meters (11,800 feet—over two miles). The subdued ridges in the bedrock floor described above are spurs of the great subglacial Gamburtsev Mountains of central East Antarctica, whose main features were discovered by earlier Soviet traverse parties. If stripped of their massive ice cover, these mountains would stand out as a range of the same magnitude as the Appalachians, but they are completely buried by the ice sheet. Not a single *nunatak* pokes above the snow surface in this whole vast section of the Antarctic continent.

It took us several days of hard shoveling to dig the station out of the drifted snow; after a few more days of fix-up work it was in full operating condition, with the generators, stoves, and radio station running smoothly. Komsomolskaya was a compact facility, containing a sleeping room for six people, generator room, combination office and radio shack, library, and bath. The library was small but well stocked with the works of Dostoyevsky, Gogol, Chekhov, and Lenin, plus a number of foreign authors, including O. Henry, and there was something eerily science-fictionlike about thawing these cultural treasures out of the glacial frost. It was particularly important to the Russians to get the *banya* in operation. As Boris Zakhariev put it, "You don't have a complete program at a station without a *Russkaya banya!*" I thoroughly agreed. It felt great to be steam-cleaned after a month and a half without bathing at all.

Dr. Shastin gave us all a thorough medical checkup. We were somewhat dehydrated because of the extremely dry air, and we definitely felt the altitude, but nobody was actually sick from it. Otherwise, everyone was in good physical condition except for a significant elevation of blood pressure that affected all of us. In Ivanov's case it was so high that the doctor advised him to return to Mirnyy on the first flight. The big man was not at all happy about this, but the doctor was adamant, and after considerable grumbling Ivanov agreed to go. He had good reason to be proud of his direction of the scientific program of the traverse, and everybody heartily sympathized with his reluctance to leave.

We were receiving a lot more news from the outside, now that Kazadaev had a proper radio station to work with. The big story was the presidential election in the United States. The Russians were very optimistic about the prospects for the incoming administration. Now that John F. Kennedy was president-elect, their previous rather negative attitudes toward him had changed. His youth suddenly became an asset instead of a liability, for it carried the promise of a much-needed fresh outlook, and his voice was considered "inspiring."

Nikita Khrushchev was on the move again, and had made his notorious shoe-pounding appearance at the United Nations. This unseemly spectacle mortified the Russians, but I consoled them with the observation that it well befitted the dignity of the international political arena. In Russia a little-known protégé of Khrushchev, Leonid Ilyich Brezhnev, had been raised to the largely titular but still prestigious post of chairman of the Supreme Soviet. This was an important symbolic move, since Brezhnev replaced Kliment Voroshilov, the last of Stalin's inner circle of cronies to retain a prominent position. Mikhail S. Gorbachev at this time was an obscure Komsomol official in his native Stavropol.

Back in Antarctica, Albert P. Crary was leading another traverse out of McMurdo, this time to the *yuzhnyy polyus* (south pole). It would be the first overland journey to the pole by an American expedition. In the Mirnyy area, the work on Pobeda Ice Island had been almost completed by Bezukladnikov and Maksakov, who was now up and around but would not be rejoining us on the traverse after all. Commo Chief Aralov also relayed a personal message from the U.S. Antarctic Projects Office to me: my replacement as exchange scientist, a physicist named Stewart Gillmor, was already aboard the *Ob* en route to Mirnyy, with a large mailbag for me. I had a foreboding that the names Stewart Gillmor and Gilbert Dewart would cause confusion for our hosts, and I was right.

Plans for the remainder of the traverse were in a state of flux. We did not yet know when we would be relieved at Komsomolskaya, which of our people would continue the trip to Vostok, or whether we still had time to attempt a return traverse. A great deal depended on the requirements of the approaching Sixth Expedition, the capabilities of the aviation section, and the availability of key personnel. Messages were shot back and forth between Mirnyy and Komsomolskaya for a couple of weeks and at last, on December 19, the position became clearer. The hoped-for return traverse was now extremely doubtful—time was just getting too short. The resupply of vital fuel to Vostok would be the sole immediate objective, and the scientific program would have to be sacrificed. Ivanov was still slated to go out on the first flight to Mirnyy, and Tsukernik and Shastin would occupy Komsomolskaya until relieved by the Sixth Expedition.

Boris Zakhariev and I had the choice of remaining at the ministation or accompanying the tractor trains the rest of the way to Vostok. We volunteered to complete the traverse, since Krasnikov could use the extra hands and I could still obtain some useful gravimetric data along the old route. The traverse party would now consist of eight men, just enough for the sleeping accommodations in the flag *balok*. With the science *balok* no longer needed, Krasnikov had us remove it from its tractor bed so that the machine would have a lighter load on the 542 kilometers (337 miles) through extremely soft snow to Vostok.

We had already begun to prepare the landing strip for the arrival of the aircraft. All the runway signs were drifted over, and the surface was too soft for safe landings, so we set out marker barrels and flags and drove the tractors up and down the strip to compact the snow. There was an old snowplow buried in the drifts near the station, but before it could be used we had to make a lot of repairs on it. Maintenance on our superannuated tractors was also taking up a lot of our time.

The weather at Komsomolskaya that December wasn't bad. The temperature generally ranged between −15° and −40° F, though it did drop to as low as −53°, and on one exceptional occasion actually rose to a summery zero. The good part was that most of the time there was mercifully little wind. We were treated to some spectacular optical phenomena produced in the cold air charged with fine ice crystals. Often the sun was surrounded by multiple concentric halos and glaring mock suns, and sometimes a second set of halos intersected the primary ones. Then the sky seemed laced with a shimmering spiderweb of pale rainbows studded with brilliant dewdrops.

Our open-ended discussion—the Great Trans-Antarctic Russian-American Seminar—continued without let-up at Komsomolskaya. The ratification of the Antarctic Treaty by the United States and the Soviet Union had been big and welcome news, and we talked about the much-desired treaty and its implications and ramifications for a long time. Could Antarctica avoid the destructive national rivalries that were tearing the rest of the world apart? Could it remain an island of peaceful cooperation for those who spoke the common international language of science? Might the treaty even become a model to be followed in other parts of the world? We hoped so, but as one man expressed our pragmatic doubts: "The Antarctic Treaty should work very well, at least until something of real commercial value is found down here to set us at loggerheads again."

With the end of the year coming up, we decided to celebrate a grand combination New Year's-Christmas-Midsummer's Day with all the trappings, and we began our preparations several days in advance. Ivanov set about creating a three foot *yolka* tree out of bits of wood, paper, and wire, which turned out to be a real work of art. We painted it an unpleasant green—it figured that the Soviets would have stashed at this remote location large supplies of that paint customarily described as "hospital green." After we had hung pillboxes, colored light bulbs, and various other trinkets on it, the Christmas tree was a very cheerful sight. Vitaly suspended strings of flashlight bulbs from the ceiling of the little station, and Yuri Birger displayed an unexpected talent by drawing a splendid poster that showed a baby, 1961, pulling our tractors and sledges into the new year. We wanted the flags of our nations to oversee the festivities, but we had no American flag, so I made one out of strips of colored paper. My mutterings about being a "bloody Betsy Ross" were lost on my comrades.

Shastin broke out the best of our remaining food for the traditional holiday repast, and it turned out that the cunning fellow had been hoarding some delicacies like caviar and crabmeat for this very occasion. There was, of course, an adequate supply of vodka, and even some champagne for the crowning moments. We did not bother to wait for the local midnight to begin the endless rounds of toasting. The cries of "Na Zdorovye!" (To your health!) started with the first arrival of the new year on the planet Earth, and the celebration was repeated every hour for twenty-four hours—or as long as the *zelenaya zmeya* (green serpent, that is, alcohol) allowed us to remain standing. We followed the progress of the meridian on a wall map of the world. (Our mathematically minded navigator, Maltsev, was naturally responsible for this.) Special toasts to international friendship and cooperation were raised when the new year came to Moscow and Washington, D.C. We sent out messages of good will, in voice and Morse code, to all the other Antarctic stations, and received many in return, including a direct call by voice from McMurdo Sound. Radio Moscow also beamed a special congratulatory broadcast to the expedition.

Meanwhile, back at Mirnyy, the *Ob* had docked at the ice front and the Sixth Expedition had begun to disembark. Our long-awaited plane finally arrived on January 8, bearing a mechanic and a radio operator from among the new personnel to help run Komsomolskaya. It also brought my first mail, but I was sorely disappointed: I received no personal letters, only official items and scientific journals.

There was a large mystery box for me from Washington marked "Urgent." This impressive-looking package was very securely wrapped, and everyone gathered around expectantly as I struggled to open it. I had visions of some wonderful new scientific device, a golden key to unlock the mysteries of the poles, but all it contained was an enormous number of totally useless computer punch cards. I sat there surrounded by wrappings and cards and thought about that stupid box being flown from Washington to Capetown, then carried in the hold of the *Ob* to Mirnyy, then flown out to our distant station at great risk and incalculable expense, and I didn't know whether to laugh or cry. This time it was Vitaly's turn to shake his head and mumble something about the inscrutable Americans.

Ivanov, who by this time was pretty much under the weather, and Shastin departed on the plane's return flight to Mirnyy, leaving Vitaly to remain at the outpost temporarily with the new men. The rest of us prepared for the final leg of our journey. At last, after what seemed a very long month of knocking around at Komsomolskaya, we revved up the diesels and headed south for Vostok on the late afternoon of January 9.

From the start, we made very slow progress through the deep, soft snow. After two days the party had gone only fifty-one kilometers from Komsomolskaya. Then we experienced the worst mechanical breakdown of the entire trip. The main clutch on one of the tractors went out, and it was back to the log and chain again. When the transmission had been torn down, it was apparent that a whole new clutch assembly would be needed, and that would have to be flown out from Mirnyy. We radioed the base about our problem, and an aircraft was got ready for the flight to the Komsomolskaya landing strip. The snow in the vicinity of the tractor trains was so soft that it would be too hazardous to attempt a landing of the long-range aircraft there.

In the meantime, our master mechanic, the skillful Ivan Bubel, who had worked harder and longer on the ailing vehicles than anybody else, was beginning to experience severe respiratory difficulties. When we drove back to the Komsomolskaya airstrip in an unhitched ATT to pick up the clutch assembly, Bubel went along, and at Dr. Shastin's insistence he was taken back to Mirnyy on the return flight. It turned out that he had frozen and dehydrated part of his lungs during those hours of labor in the desiccating cold, and the doctors ordered him to take it easy for a while. Ivan Bubel was to be sorely missed.

We got the engine back together, but we continued to have a great deal of trouble with the deep, soft snow that covers this part of the ice sheet. The tractors often sank in over the tops of their tracks, and frequently they bogged down into total immobility. The drivers sometimes resorted to running them backwards for better traction, but this made them overheat, and it also gave one an uneasy feeling of retrogression to watch the odometer subtracting kilometers instead of adding them. Occasionally we had to hitch up two tractors in tandem to pull one sledge, then double back to pick up the other two sledges one at a time, a frustratingly slow, laborious process.

The route between Komsomolskaya and Vostok lies across the most desolate region in the world. It is part of the vast desert of central Antarctica, where the precipitation is less than two inches of water equivalent per year. By an odd numerical coincidence, the temperature on the Fahrenheit scale drops about as far below zero here (and at about the same time) as it goes above it in that other great desert, the Sahara. Vostok Station was already established as the coldest known spot in the world, and on August 24, 1960, a new world's record low had been set there: $-88.3°$ C ($-126.9°$ F). Until recently, this huge, frozen expanse was described as being as unknown as "the far side of the moon." Odd, too, that its exploration should be nearly simultaneous with that of the earth's orbiting neighbor.

Murphy's famous law was in full force on this leg of the traverse—if anything could go wrong, it would—and I discovered that there is a Russian counterpart, the *Zakon Mirovogo Blyetsva*, which translates loosely as the "Law of Universal Contrariness." It has certain corollaries, one of which is that natural forces will combine against you to thwart your efforts, even if they must violate the laws of probability to do it. We did indeed seem to be having more than our share of bad luck with the rolling stock. First a gearbox blew up, then a generator burned out, a fly-wheel developed a crack, and a track broke. Insult was added to injury when one of the massive steel couplings by which the sledges were hitched broke off completely and we had to make up a new coupling unit out of cable and chain. I was beginning to think that *remont* was the most common word in the Russian language. It was not some mysterious law that was working, however, just the effects of high stresses at low temperatures on old and much-used equipment.

Each of us had regular tasks. Mine was melting snow for our water supply with a cantankerous old stove taken from a preheating system for aircraft engines. It was a devil to start, but once I had it going on the sunny side of the *balok* and out of the wind, it created a sphere of warmth that was, as the Russians say, like Tashkent. One of the most onerous of the daily chores, which I shared with Zakhariev and Kantuev, was replacing the steel pins that held the interlocking plates of the tracks together. These pins sheared off frequently under the stress of plowing through the deep snow, and they had to be replaced before they worked loose and the track separated. Every few hours we would stop and inspect the tracks. The pins that had failed since the last stop were removed and new ones inserted. This involved driving the defective pin out with a sledge hammer and steel rod, then climbing under the tractor and driving the rod back out with the new pin. The second part was the tough job because you had to wield the heavy hammer while lying on your back in the barely passable crawl space between the snow surface and the bottom of the chassis. The discomfort of this job was aggravated by the rarefied atmosphere—breathing became rapid and raspingly labored, and an excruciating headache throbbed with each pulse beat. I felt as if we were driving a meter of steel through those tracks for every meter of our route.

I thought then of the legendary John Henry driving steel through that West Virginia mountain, and I translated the stirring old folk ballad into Russian for my partners. They read a lot of their own poignant meanings into that epic of man against machine. Meanwhile, we had been making up our own song about our work, a piece of earthy doggerel entitled "Tam byl glavnyy friktsion" (There was a main clutch).

Sometimes it's uncanny how a man's name fits his function. Law and order were enforced in the Klondike gold rush by a case-hardened officer of the Northwest Mounted Police named Sam Steele. General Eisenhower's name, which means "iron-cutter" in German, must have sounded ominous to the Wehrmacht. Our leader's name was Krasnikov, and *krasnyy* means "red." Red both in his florid complexion and in the Russian political sense he certainly was—an animated fountainhead of slogans and maxims. Every morning he would have us fall out in front of the tractors and give us a little pep talk on what we were going to accomplish for the Fatherland that day. I felt embarrassed at first, like an outsider who wanders into Knute Rockne's locker room during halftime. My anomalous presence among the troops didn't seem to bother Krasnikov a bit, however, and the daily pep rally soon lost its novelty for me. After a while it became like so many other things that had seemed strange before but were now just part of the game.

Those who had crossed the plateau before had warned us of a symptom that was now becoming serious—loss of interest in food. To make things worse, we were running out of the goodies that had stimulated our flagging appetites. When we approached the end of our supply of *pelmeni* and fruitcake an ancient Russian custom was revived, the *razdeleniye* (dividing up) of scarce rations. We entered into this little ritual with something close to glee. I wondered if this was how the Cossacks had shared their booty, or the peasants the land in the village communes of old Russia. Russians have a deep feeling for what is fair by their standards. It embraces a spectrum that ranges from warmhearted charity for those who have been unjustly treated to implacable retribution on the doers of injustice.

In our spare time we amused ourselves with dominoes and chess, played with great intensity on tiny boards, and with card games, which were more in favor here than back at Mirnyy. I taught the Russians to play bouré, a Cajun card game that has been carried to the uttermost parts of the earth by the doddlebugging fraternity. Our driver-mechanics passed the time with word games that were much too intellectual for me, such as identifying the composers of operas and symphonies.

Although it was getting colder now as the brief austral summer slid away, we were still blessed by a lack of wind. On some days it was almost preternaturally calm. The diesel smoke remained just where it had come out of the stacks, and you could look back and see the long, thin black clouds hovering over the snow and marking our trail for many kilometers. Early in February the temperature hit one of those magic numbers, $-50°$ C ($-58°$ F), below which extreme caution is to be exercised, wind or no wind. Heat loss from the skin is so rapid that frostbite occurs when it has been exposed for only a few minutes. This part of the route had been driven before, and every so often we would sight an empty fuel drum left by one of the previous tractor parties, like a buoy on a frozen ocean.

We were beginning to look pretty haggard and were feeling the fatigue of the journey in our bones. A lot of irritability and exasperation came out, but we had also developed a feeling of closeness that both bound us together and excluded the rest of the world. The insular community of a traverse party or an isolated station becomes very close-knit, with its own strong sense of identity and loyalty. In a massively staged expedition like Operation Deepfreeze or its Soviet equivalent, the advance field units are bound to clash sooner or later with the support services in the base area—the rear echelon, in military parlance. It has been my sad experience that this built-in antagonism is usually ignored or underestimated by administrators, whether American bureaucrats or Soviet apparatchiki. Quite a few discouraging words crackled over the airwaves between our roving repair shop and the Mirnyy Pentagon.

We finally made it to Vostok on the eighth of February. All the station personnel, including Sidorov and a few other holdovers from the Fifth Expedition, turned out to greet us. Sidorov presented a bottle of champagne to Krasnikov, who solemnly poured a drink for each of us. Vitaly was there, having flown up from Komsomolskaya shortly after the Sixth Expedition relief team arrived. He gave us the news that the return traverse was now definitely canceled, and our only remaining scientific project was a final seismic measurement near Vostok. Vitaly had the seismic sounding gear all ready, but the shooting had to wait until new batteries were flown up from Mirnyy. Most of the traverse party and the last of the old Vostok crew were to go back on the next flight, and the rest of us on the one after that.

We had all lost a lot of weight on the final phase of the traverse. The food, though plentiful, had seemed tasteless, and, as I noted above, we had no desire to eat it. Now our appetites abruptly returned. I can still remember the overwhelming aroma of the freshly baked black bread in the Vostok galley, and how delicious it tasted after the thawed-out stale loaves that we had been munching on for months. My companions had often remarked that I wasn't much of a bread eater, but at Vostok I amazed them and myself by gorging on it. Shastin was moved to write a medical paper on the physical and psychological aspects of this behavior.

Vostok was a very small station, and like Komsomolskaya, it was nearly covered by drifted snow. The entrance tunnel was lined with shelves of frozen food, much of it of very good quality. Vostok, in view of its isolation and severe weather, was considered an extreme hardship post, and everything was done to make life there as bearable as it could be. With the Fifth and Sixth Expedition people there, plus the traverse party, it was overcrowded, so we continued to live out in the flag *balok*, though we took our meals in the general mess hall. The temperature was sixty below or lower nearly every day now, and the first man up in the morning had to exert a good deal of willpower to extract himself from his warm sleeping bag and dash over to light the stove. We had a spell of unusually breezey weather around the middle of February (it wasn't supposed to blow that hard in the deep interior of Antarctica) and the combination of low temperature and wind made it impossible to keep the creaking old hulk warm.

Parked near the station were the Kharkovchanka tractors that had been used in the south pole traverse of the previous year. These huge, sleek machines looked a lot like the Snow Cruiser that Admiral Byrd brought to the Antarctic in 1940 in a bid to revolutionize polar travel with a self-contained exploration vehicle. (Ernest Shackleton had introduced motor transport to the continent in 1907. This vehicle gave out after the first two miles of the great journey that eventually attained the south magnetic pole.) Unfortunately, the Snow Cruiser proved unable to overcome the difficult snow surface conditions on the Ross Ice Shelf near Little America. The Kharkovchanka was reasonably successful, but I understood that it too had its frailties. One feature about it that really appealed to me was that it had a trap door in the floor through which a gravimeter could be lowered for reading. My nose was still sore and peeling from the few unpleasant times when it had frozen to the metal on the eyepiece of my meter. But because of the difficulties of making gravimetric measurements from a tractor, this innovation was not always practical.

After we had unloaded our precious cargo of fuel and deposited the drums in the depot by the airstrip, we fell into the regular routine of life at the station, helping with chores like digging snow for the watermaker, improving the runway, and building a new latrine. We began to empathize with what might be called the "outpost syndrome" of the inhabitants, the sense of manning a Roman fort or a Chinese wall, of being at the ultimate limit of civilization. Some features of the lonely base were unique, like the breathing gear specially designed to protect the respiratory system during the overwhelming cold of midwinter. This was a suit not unlike a deep-sea diver's, which drew air into the helmet past the relatively warm body of the wearer.

We were maintaining excellent radio communication with Mirnyy, and I was able to talk directly to my replacement, Stewart Gillmor. He was settling in all right at the base and didn't seem to have any real problems, except that the Russians were swamped by the three tons of electronic equipment he had brought along for his studies of the upper atmosphere. A friendly, easygoing fellow with a lot of ingenuous curiosity, he was getting along very well with his hosts. He had some good news about the American Expedition: Bert Crary's traverse party had reached the south pole on February 17. Naturally, that event called for a major celebration at Vostok. We also learned that the changeover at Mirnyy from the Fifth to the Sixth Expedition was now well under way, and the *Ob* was expected to leave for home early in March. The plane arrived and departed, bringing our precious batteries to power the seismic equipment and evacuating the rest of the Vostok crew and the traverse party, except for Tsukernik, Zakhariev, and me.

Vitaly, Boris, and I got off our last seismic shot on February 18. Vostok lies at an elevation of 3,488 meters (11,440 feet), and we bounced an echo off the bedrock at about sea level, so that altitude represented the thickness of the ice sheet. At 78° 27′ south, 106° 52′ east, Vostok is at about the latitude, in the Northern Hemisphere, of Spitsbergen (Svalbard). Spitsbergen, however, is an archipelago in the Arctic Ocean, whereas here, at the south geomagnetic pole, we were deep in the middle of a continent. This antisymmetry of the poles is one of the fascinating puzzles of earth's configuration.

Now we waited impatiently from day to day for our flight back to Mirnyy, but after the brief window of navigability around the seventeenth the elements seemed to conspire against us. Every time a flight could be scheduled the weather would be bad at either Mirnyy or Vostok or, if the only plane available was an LI-2, which had to make an intermediate refueling stop at Komsomolskaya because of its short range, the weather would be foul there. Murphy's law was still very much in effect. The nagging worry was growing in the back of our minds: suppose the weather never does break and the ship has to leave without us?

But at last, on February 25, one day over four months after the tractor trains had roared out of Mirnyy, our flying salvation touched down at the Vostok airstrip. We shouted our farewells to the new occupants of Vostok, boarded the aircraft, and, with an indescribable feeling of relief, flew back to the main base.

10

Do Svidoniya!

A solitary sail that rises
White in the blue mist on the foam,
What is it in far lands it prizes?
What does it leave behind at home?
— *Mikhail Lermontov*

Upon our return from Vostok, Vitaly, Boris, and I were met at the
Mirnyy aerodrome by Korotkevich, Venediktov, Ivanov, Maksakov,
and Stewart Gillmor. The Russians later remarked on the cold ca-
sualness (no hugging and kissing in the Russian style) with which
Gillmor and I met—after all, I hadn't seen another of my compatriots
in fourteen months—so I explained about the stiff-upper-lip tradition of undemonstrativeness among Western explorers. "Ah, yes,"
said one of my friends with a gleam of recognition, "like your Henry
M. Stanley and his 'Dr. Livingstone, I presume!' "

Everybody at Mirnyy, Gillmor included, looked a litle strange to
us, but not so strange as we did to them, I'll warrant, with our scraggly
beards, our gaunt, sunburned faces, and our numbed reactions. We
must have resembled a band of ancient Russian monks just back from
a penitential sojourn in the Siberian wilderness.

At this time I noticed an attitude at Mirnyy that was familiar to me
from the changeover at Wilkes Station three years before: resistance
on the part of the old-timers toward the newcomers. After the effusive

176

(and sincere) initial greetings a vague impression, that these outland-
ers were intruders in "our" camp, developed, and it took several days
to dissipate. A year of isolation had bred a sense of unity that tran-
scended any personal differences among us. The formal ceremony of
handing over the station and legitimizing its new "owners" was not
just an empty ritual; it filled a real human need.

The scientific field team reported back to the Pentagon on the results of the traverse. Korotkevich was there, with Venediktov, Matveychuk, and V. M. Driatski, the recently arrived leader of the Sixth
Expedition. This was my last visit to the expedition headquarters. We
had our successes to relate, including the wide jog into previously
unexplored territory between Mirnyy and Komsomolskaya. We also
had regrets that we had not been able to do more, but everybody
realized that not much more could have been done with the equipment at hand, the staggering logistical demands made upon us, and
the merciless limits of time. In any event, it was all over now. The
disagreements that had burned up the airwaves a short time before
were all but forgotten. At the end of our long discussion we all sat
back and looked around at each other with the unspoken understanding of finality, conscious of our part in the international saga of polar
exploration, a quest for knowledge and a quest for peace; conscious
that we had done the very best we could. We were also sadly aware
that if things had gone differently another man, Oskar Krichak,
would certainly have been there with us that day, asking excitedly
about such matters as the weather conditions on the polar plateau,
and cracking some terrible puns and hilarious jokes.

While we were struggling across the high plateau of central Antarctica, valuable scientific studies were being carried out at Lazarev Station and its vicinity. In addition to Bokanenko's successful investigation of the ice shelf there, the geologists had found a real treasure
trove in the interior. In the course of a far-flung aerial reconnaissance
survey, one of the senior pilots, Barabanov, had flown through a pass
in the mountains south of Lazarev and discovered an extensive area
of exposed rock. Solovyev and the other geologists had eagerly plunged
in to explore it. The Russians now had a strong motive to maintain
their presence in that area.

My voluminous accumulation of mail provided me with a chronicle of the events of the past year, many forgettable, but some touching

me profoundly. Beno Gutenberg, the grand old man of geophysics, had died recently. He had retired as director of Caltech's Seismological Laboratory shortly before I went to work there, but he still came in to his office every day and continued his research. He had always been most gracious to me in his courtly Old-World manner, and he had shown a keen interest in my Antarctic project. He had asked me to trace the route of the expedition on his huge globe, and he had put questions to me that still remain unanswered. Another recent death that struck home was that of a personal hero, Roy Chapman Andrews, the former director of the American Museum of Natural History and leader of its expeditions to Central Asia. I did not know him personally, but his fascinating writings about exploration and science and the marvelous museum he administered had strongly influenced me in my choice of career, and we had corresponded briefly before I left on the Soviet expedition.

Not all the news was of such a somber nature. "Dyadya Gil" had become an uncle for the second time, and there were baby pictures to show around. This delighted the Russians, who will whip out their wallets and show you snapshots of their families at the slightest provocation. We soon had a "welcome home to Mirnyy" party, at which wife-and-children photos that had recently come in the mail were passed around proudly. To this shindig Gillmor contributed some fine old Kentucky bourbon, which proved extremely popular. For some reason, iron-throated sons of the steppes who could put away enormous quantities of vodka without flinching were quickly floored by American whiskey. It was a great party.

Stew Gillmor, who had been working in the San Francisco Bay area before joining the expedition, admitted that he was nonplussed when he arrived at Mirnyy to hear Shelley Manne and his Men on the station P.A. system and see people wandering around reading the *Evergreen Review*. The infectious quality of American culture in both its positive and negative aspects never ceases to amaze even Americans.

Stew had some interesting tales to tell of the past year, one of which activated a delayed buzzer in my mind. A while back, my friendly enemy the base commander had informed me, with smug satisfaction, that there had been an "insurrection" in San Francisco. I discounted this report, though I thought at the time that there was no more likely place for one. Now along came Gillmor to confirm it, at least in part. He had been there. The incident in question was the May 1960 demonstration at City Hall against the hearings of the House Un-American Activities Committee, involving the "hosing down" of dissident students by the police. This was a tame event by the standards of the decade to follow, but I've heard people in academia date it as the beginning of the turbulent Sixties.

Before I had left on the traverse I had dispatched to Washington a long list of items that I recommended my successor as exchange scientist should bring along, things that would be useful to him and interesting to the Russians. It included hobby magazines, mail-order catalogues and hand tools (the do-it-yourself boom was just hitting the United States, and the Soviet Union could use it). I was gratified that most of the requested material arrived in Gillmor's mountain of baggage. Unfortunately for him, however, none of the food for making snacks had been sent, and the following winter Stew was to have tantalizing dreams about peanut-butter sandwiches (the Russians were vaguely aware of but didn't quite understand the role of the peanut in the American Way of Life).

After the sterility of the interior plateau, Mirnyy seemed to seethe with life. Its summer population of about two hundred was metropolitan to us, and the animal life along the shore and in the skies was overwhelming. The coastal weather felt almost tropical. The late summer temperature was about thirty above at Mirnyy, while it had been −64° F at Vostok the day before we had left. In the aviation age you are whisked so abruptly from one milieu to another that you are likely to develop a case of cultural bends along with your physical jet lag, and my companions and I were stunned by being suddenly plunged into the frenetic activity of organizing and packing our research materials and other returnable items for the voyage home. At least Mirnyy, unlike U.S. stations in summer, was not plagued by a procession of visiting VIPs.

We had anticipated that there just might be a woman or two among the personnel of the Sixth Expedition. Rumors had abounded that the Russians were going to break the sex barrier and send female scientists to the Antarctic in 1961. These proved to be unfounded. According to the grapevine, a highly qualified woman had indeed demanded a place on the expedition and had made quite an issue of sex discrimination, but her application had been conveniently "lost" in the bureaucratic maze. The hidebound Soviet establishment was not ready for such a radical move at that time (nor was ours).

We had also hoped that the huge new *ledokol* (icebreaker) *Lenin*, the first surface ship ever to be powered by atomic energy, would visit Mirnyy after its shakedown cruise in the north. However, again according to the grapevine, she was apparently having problems with her nuclear reactor. A major advance in Antarctic air travel had been made, however, by the Americans, who had introduced the C-130 Hercules aircraft in 1960; the "Herc," a rugged, four-engine prop-jet with great range and cargo capacity, soon became the workhorse of the American program. The arrival of this mighty new logistical instrument appropriately coincided with the decision on the part of both superpowers to make the Antarctic effort into a continuing, open-ended endeavor.

After the solemn ceremonies and the lighthearted going-away parties, the *Ob* sailed out into the Davis Sea on March 12. She was scheduled to arrive at Capetown on March 29 and at her home port, Leningrad, on April 28. Many of my friends had invited me to visit them in Russia during their three-month postexpedition vacation, and I tried to arrange to go back with them, but somewhere in the bureaucratic tangle between Washington and Moscow my request had run into trouble, and it was, not altogether unexpectedly, denied. I did not get to visit the Soviet Union for several years, but when I did, I found that it conformed perfectly to my mental image of it.

We scientific personnel were kept busy on the voyage transcribing technical data from field notebooks to permanent records and exchanging it among ourselves. As it turned out, we should have done more exchanging, because as cooperative as the individual Russians clearly wanted to be, the red tape involved in getting data out of the Soviet Union later proved in many cases to be as insurmountable as it had been in trying to get me in. However, they did publish an article I wrote for their expedition bulletin about ice/rock layering of the earth's crust in Antarctica.

Captain Sviridov, the *Ob*'s skipper, was a renowned polar navigator, and he was also a gracious host. I took part in an English class, as I had aboard the *Kooperatsiya* on the way down, and it was certainly no chore, since the class was enlivened by the attendance of two attractive young ladies from the ship's crew. Maybe it was just the after-effect of coming off the ice, but I was sure that the women were more stylishly dressed than they been the year before. Undoubtedly there had been some changes. At a party in which I gave my final appearance before a Russian audience—singing "Oh, Susannah!" with a balalaika quartet accompaniment—some of the off-duty crew members showed up in Levis and cowboy shirts.

After a year spent in a totally male society, it was marvelous to realize that women really do exist in the world. A little in-joke among our group became the subject of a cartoon, which was posted on the ship's bulletin board (no doubt to the mystification of many who saw it). After noting that the population of the United States derives from all over the world, one of my friends had asked me to compare the charms of the women of different nationalities. I parried this question in good Khrushchevian style with a well-known quotation from Lenin (which originally had a political context), "In the dark, all cats are gray!" Hence the cartoon of a grinning, gray Cheshire cat that faintly resembled the American comrade, with the inscription, "Ladies, beware!"

Once again, we found the Southern Ocean virtually empty of other shipping. Our closest neighbors were a couple of large whaling fleets, Soviet and Japanese, with which we exchanged weather data. Antarctic whaling was just entering into a marked decline as the result of overkilling during the whaling boom of the late 1940s and 1950s, and the International Whaling Commission was beginning to look at the ecological problems of the industry in an unprecedentedly serious way. It was an important step in the worldwide development of environmental awareness.

The *Ob* steamed into Capetown a day ahead of schedule. She had three days in port, and my comrades had plenty of shore leave this time. I had promised to remain in town until the *Ob* departed in case I could be of any help in dealing with the locals. Caltech had wired money to the U.S. consulate for my trip home, plus expenses, and I was left to make whatever travel and baggage shipping arrangements I chose. My freedom of action in such matters as international travel was all but incomprehensible and gallingly enviable to the Russians.

The Cold War lost little time in rearing its icy head. On my first visit to the consulate I was ushered into the presence of an official who had

been sketchily filled in on my background, and whose opening remark was, "Well, how did those bastards treat you?" I was so dumb-
founded at the classification of my mates as "bastards" that there was
a delay before I became angry. To this apparatchik, Russians—any
Russians—could be considered only as adversaries. To me, my particular Russians were people to whom I would gladly entrust my life,
as in fact I had.

I continued to stay pretty close to my Russian friends for the remainder of the expedition ship's stay in Capetown. We did a lot of
shopping together, and I logged a considerable amount of translating
in department stores and tourist traps. On this stopover the returning
expedition members were allowed to wander about the city on their
own, and they had been allotted a fair amount of foreign currency to
spend, though it never seemed enough to them in those shops bulging
with tempting goodies. Although Soviet Russia and South Africa
were at each other's throats diplomatically at that time over the crisis
in the Congo, my shipmates and I (I was naturally assumed to be a
Russian by the townsfolk) were treated with great friendliness wherever we went. I think that the high point of the visit was a leisurely
afternoon with my closest friends sitting on the veranda of a delight-
ful old Victorian hotel, sipping tall, cool drinks, and reminiscing
about the myriad events of our recent so very different past in a very
different world.

All too soon my companions were leaving, and I was down at the
same old dock, seeing them off. I found myself back aboard the ship
being hugged and kissed—Russians are not at all inhibited at such
times of high emotion—and then thrown bodily into the air several
times to cries of "Urrah! Urrah!" Then the *Ob*'s piercing whistle blew,
and I was carried down the gangway by a mob of my whooping and
hollering colleagues. While the mooring lines were cast off and the
ship eased slowly away from the pier, a shower of gifts was thrown to
me, including a toy animal with a tag that read "For President
Kennedy's children and for peace." As the *Ob* moved farther away the
crowd on her rail started chanting in unison, "Do Svidoniya! . . .
Goodbye . . . Do Svidoniya . . . Goodbye!"

At last the *Ob* was only a speck at the end of the breakwater, as the
Kooperatsiya had been when I waited in curious anticipation on the
same spot fifteen months before. That evening I wrote of my state of

mind in a letter to my parents: "Then I was alone, and, believe me, I felt alone, after a year of hardship and happiness, of work and comradeship and tragedy, with these wonderful people."

Another Antarctic adventure was over.

Glossary

Ablation. The removal of ice, snow, or water from a glacier or other natural ice or snow feature, by any means, including evaporation, melting, wind transport, calving, and avalanching.

Accumulation. The addition of ice, snow, or water to a glacier or other natural ice or snow feature, by any means, including precipitation (snow, rain, hail), condensation from vapor (hoarfrost), and wind transport.

Adelie penguin. The smaller and much more common of the two truly Antarctic species of penguins. These gregarious, flightless birds are highly specialized for marine life; they summer on the Antarctic coast and winter in the pack ice.

Altitude sickness. Various symptoms associated with the deficiency of oxygen at high altitudes: lethargy, loss of appetite, weakness, nausea, dizziness.

Antarktida. Antarctica.

AN-2. Antonov-2. A durable, maneuverable, single-engine biplane employed in Soviet polar operations. Designed by O. K. Antonov. (Soviet aircraft types are named after the aeronautical engineer who designed them.)

Apparatchik. Strictly speaking, a career official in the permanent Communist party *apparat* (staff); loosely, any bureaucrat, with unfavorable connotations.

ATT. Artilleriiskiy Tyagach Tyazhelyy. A heavy artillery prime mover.

Aurora. Colorful displays in the night sky in the polar regions. Atomic particles from the sun, channeled by the earth's magnetic field, collide with oxygen and nitrogen molecules in the upper atmosphere, releasing

185

visible energy. The aurora borealis is centered around the north geomagnetic pole and the aurora australis around the south geomagnetic
pole.

Austral.   Southern; pertaining to the southern hemisphere.

Banya.   Russian steam bath.

Balok.   Mobile hut or shelter mounted on a tractor, sledge or trailer. Equivalent to the American *wanigan*.

Belay.   In mountaineering practice, roping a climber so as to prevent or
shorten a fall and reduce its hazardous effects.

Beset.   Said of a vessel so tightly surrounded by sea ice that it cannot control
its movements.

Brash.   Floating fragments of ice in the sea less than two meters across, from
any source.

Bumagi.   Papers; documents; identification.

Burya.   Storm, gale.

Calving.   The breaking off of a piece of ice from an ice shelf, glacier, or
iceberg; the process by which icebergs are formed from an ice shelf or
glacier front.

Chairman.   Russian *predsedatel*; the chairman of the Council of Ministers
is the chief executive officer in the Soviet state, comparable to a premier
or prime minister. Nikita S. Khrushchev was chairman from 1958 to
1964.

Climatology.   The study of climate and the causes of its variations locally
and worldwide. (Extention of this study back through geologic time,
e.g., to the Pleistocene Ice Age, is called *paleoclimatology*.)

Commo.   American military slang for communications.

Convergence.   The meeting of ocean currents or water masses having different properties. The Antarctic Convergence is indicated by a marked
change in water surface temperature.

Crust.   The outermost layer of the earth, significantly different in its physical properties from the denser material that lies below it (the *mantle*).
The crust under the continents averages about thirty-five kilometers
(twenty-two miles) thick, while the oceanic crust is only about five kilometers (three miles) thick.

Cult of personality.   Name applied by critics to Josef Stalin's doctrine that
history is made by the great individual leader (e.g., himself), and that the
masses count for little; the reverse of Marxism.

Cyrillic.   The Russian alphabet, borrowed and transmuted from Greek and
Latin. Traditionally attributed to St. Cyril, ninth-century Greek mis-
sionary to the Slavs, and modified under Peter the Great and the Soviet
government.

Davis Sea. Extension of the Southern Ocean between the Shackleton Ice Shelf and West Ice Shelf and the coast of Antarctica. It was discovered in 1912 by John King Davis, captain of Douglas Mawson's expedition ship *Aurora.*

Dialectic. A philosophic viewpoint espoused by many philosophers including Karl Marx. It emphasizes the dynamic processes of change, growth, decay, and development as inherent qualities of nature, and sees all phenomena as interrelated parts of an organic continuum.

Doodlebugging. Geophysical field work; especially, prospecting for minerals using geophysical methods.

Drifting snow. Snow carried by the wind to a low height. Visibility at eye level is not significantly affected by drifting snow.

Electrical shot-firing. Initiated by engaging a blasting machine (exploder) that sends a current through an electrical blasting cap (detonator), in which the heat from a resistance wire ignites a heat-sensitive charge. The exploding cap detonates the main charge either directly or through an intermediate primer charge. This precisely timed method of firing explosives is used in the seismic exploration of sub-surface geological structures.

Emperor penguin. The larger and rarer of the two truly Antarctic penguin species. In contrast to the smaller Adelie, the Emperor winters on the coast and summers in the pack.

Entropy. A quantity in thermodynamics that reflects the degree of randomness or disorder in a system involving energy or information. According to the Second Law of Thermodynamics, there is a general tendency toward increasing entropy, i.e., greater disorder, in the universe. Higher degrees of order can be achieved locally, but only at the cost of sacrifices elsewhere.

Familiya. Last or family name.

Firn. Transitional substance between snow and glacier ice; firn is older and denser than snow but still permeable to water and thus not fully transformed into ice.

Floe. A relatively flat piece of drifting sea ice more than twenty meters (sixty-five feet) across.

Frazil. Needle-like spicules or fine discs of ice suspended in water.

Frostbite. Freezing of body tissues, commonly in the fingers, toes and face, that occurs when an extremity loses heat faster than it can be replaced by blood circulation, as when exposed to deep cold or high wind. If the condition is prolonged and unattended, the affected part may be lost. Symptoms are whitening of the skin and numbness, and treatment is by moderate and nonabrasive warming.

Geodesy.   The determination of the size and shape of the earth, its gravitational field, and the precise location of points on its surface.

Geomagnetic poles.   The projection to the earth's surface of the axis of a dipole (bar) magnet which best approximates earth's magnetic effect. Because the earth is not a perfect bar magnet, the geomagnetic poles do not coincide with the magnetic (dip) poles; however, from space the approximation is very close, and such upper atmospheric phenomena as the aurora are associated with the geomagnetic poles.

Geomagnetism.   The study of the magnetic phenomena exhibited by the earth.

Geophone.   An instrument used to pick up seismic wave energy and transform it into an electrical signal for recording by a seismograph; also called a seismometer or a "jug."

Geophysics.   The application of the principles of physics to geological problems and to the study of the earth as a planet. Branches include seismology, geodesy and gravimetry, oceanography, meteorology, and geomagnetism.

Glaciology.   The study of all forms of existing glaciers and of their characteristics and processes; in a broad sense, the study of all aspects of ice and snow. Glaciology is interdisciplinary in that it involves coordinated investigations from several scientific fields.

Glavsevmorput.   Abbreviation for the (Soviet) Northern Sea Route Administration.

Gondwanaland.   Theoretical protocontinent of the Southern Hemisphere, named for the Gondwana rocks of India, which have features, including evidence of ancient glaciation, similar to those of the now widely separated southern continents.

Gravimeter.   Instrument for measuring variations in gravitational attraction; gravity meter.

Great Northern Expedition.   A series of expeditions (1725–42) initiated by Czar Peter I ("The Great") (1672–1725) to explore the geographical relationship of Asia to North America. Commanded by the Danish mariner Vitus Bering, the expeditions explored the strait and sea that bear his name and discovered the Aleutian Islands and Alaska.

Gusenitsa.   Caterpillar; endless belt track of a tractor.

Hypothermia.   Lowering of the core temperature of the human body by cold, dampness, wind, or fatigue with resulting diminution of body functions. Inner body temperature below 95° F can be fatal. Since onset of hypothermia is usually unnoticed by the victim, the "buddy system" is imperative for people in conditions of severe exposure.

Iceberg.   A large piece of floating (or stranded) ice of any shape that has broken off from a glacier. By definition it rises more than five meters (sixteen feet) above the waterline (if smaller, it is called a "bergy bit"), and most of its mass (4/5 to 8/9) is submerged.

Icebreaker. A stoutly built, powerfully propelled, highly maneuverable ship designed to open a channel through sea ice by sliding its bow up on the ice and breaking it down with its weight.

Ice island. A large tabular iceberg.

Ice sheet. A large area of continuous glacier ice overlying a land surface; when a significant part of a continent is covered, this is called a continental glacier.

Ice shelf. The floating extension of a continental or inland ice sheet beyond the coastline.

IGY. International Geophysical Year. The period from July 1957 through December 1958, when sixty-six nations cooperated in scientific studies of the physical properties of the earth, its atmosphere, and the neighboring region of space.

IL-12. A long-range, twin-engine cargo plane designed by S. V. Ilyushin.

Isostatic. Referring to *isostasy*, the condition of gravitational equilibrium of the earth's crust by which it floats on the underlying, denser mantle. Removal of material from the crust, as by the retreat of glaciers, causes it to rebound, as a ship rises when unloaded.

Jamesway Hut. A readily assembled prefabricated structure made of wooden arches and insulated covers. Used by the U.S. military in cold climates.

Jug hustler. Worker on U.S. seismic field party who lays out and picks up the spread of geophones (jugs) and connecting cables.

KAPSh. Karkasnaya Arkticheskaya Palatka Shaposhnikova. An Arctic frame tent designed by the engineer Shaposhnikov.

Kasha. Porridge; especially, buckwheat cereal.

Kayut-kompaniya. A mess hall or wardroom.

KGB. Committee for State Security, the Soviet secret police, and much more. Like the Oprichnina (bodyguard) of Czar Ivan IV ("The Terrible") (1530–84), on which it was modeled with exacting attention to detail, the KGB is a state within a state, with a wide range of security, political, and intelligence functions.

Kharkovchanka. Large, self-contained Soviet over-snow vehicle.

Kholod. Cold.

Killer whale. Toothed whale, largest of the dolphin family, found worldwide and common in Antarctic waters. The killer whale is a powerful predator up to thirty feet long; it hunts in packs and will attack large seals and other whales.

Komsomol. Young Communist League. The political organization preparing youths and young adults for membership in the Communist party.

KPSS. Communist party of the Soviet Union, sole legal political party in the U.S.S.R., and the arena in which conflicts of interest and power are fought out. Nikita S. Khrushchev held the leading position in the party (first secretary) from 1953 to 1964.

Lager. Camp; bivouac.

Lebensraum. Concept of population pressure used by the Nazis to justify territorial expansion. (German: living space.)

Led. Ice.

Lednik. Glacier.

Ledokol. Icebreaker.

LI-2. Medium-range, twin-engine cargo plane designed by B. P. Lisunov.

Lifeline. Line of rope serving as a route guide or to mark the limits of a safe area for personnel in conditions of severe weather and poor visibility.

Luddites. English workers of the early nineteenth century who protested the inhuman conditions of the industrial revolution by destroying machinery.

Lysenkoism. Use of scientific fraud to support the miraculous claims of the Stalin cult; hence, any fabrication, suppression, or falsification of data. (After T. D. Lysenko.)

Magnetic (dip) poles. Shifting points on the earth's surface to which the north- and south-seeking poles of a compass needle point, and where the earth's magnetic lines of force are vertical (the dip or inclination is 90°). The south magnetic pole was first reached by a party led by Australian professor of geology T. W. Edgeworth David of the Shackleton Expedition in 1909.

Magnetometer. An instrument for measuring the strength of the magnetic field of the Earth (or other astronomical body).

MI-4. Large cargo helicopter (*vertolet*) designed by M. L. Mil.

Nachalnik. Leader; chief; manager.

Nachalstvo. The managerial hierarchy; supervisory personnel as a group; command cadre.

New tectonics. A theoretical model of the earth in which its surface is divided into a number of plates floating on a viscous underlayer like ice floes on the sea. Movements of the plates are powered by the process of sea-floor spreading, and their collisions account for mountain-building, volcanism, earthquakes, and other geological phenomena. The new tectonics incorporates some of the ideas of continental drift proposed by German scientist and explorer Alfred Wegener in 1912. Also called "plate tectonics."

Northern Sea route. The northeast passage through the Arctic Ocean along the coast of Siberia. Open to navigation in the summer, it is the shortest route between Soviet ports in Europe and the Far East. The entire route was first sailed by Swedish geologist Nils A. E. Nordenskiold in 1878–79.

Nunatak. An isolated hill or ridge of bedrock that projects above the surface of a glacier and is completely surrounded by ice. (Eskimo: lonely peak.)

Operation Barbarossa. Adolf Hitler's code name for the Nazi invasion of the Soviet Union on June 22, 1941.

Operation Deepfreeze. The U.S. Navy's preparatory and support operations for the American expeditions in Antarctica during IGY and afterward. Operation Deepfreeze I began in December 1955.

Operation Highjump. U.S. naval expedition to Antarctica in 1946–47. Wide-ranging aerial reconnaissance flights were made by seaplanes and from a base at Little America.

Otryad. Section; detachment; organizational unit.

Pack. An area of drifting sea ice, covering the sea surface with little or no open water, and unattached to the shore (sea ice attached to a shore or an ice shelf is called "fast ice").

Palatka. Tent.

Pancake Ice. More or less circular pieces of newly formed sea ice (diameter from thirty centimeters to three meters and thickness up to ten centimeters) with slightly raised rims from the pieces' striking against one another; also called "lily pad ice" when the pieces are small.

Pelmeni. Small dumplings filled with ground meat and spices; a Siberian delicacy.

Permian. Period in geological history from approximately 280 to 230 million years ago. The Permian was a time of intense upheaval—mountain building (e.g., the Appalachians), episodes of widespread glaciation in the Southern Hemisphere, and major changes in life forms. The presence of the fossil fern glossopteris in Permian strata of Antarctica and all the other southern continents has been cited as further evidence that they were united at that time (see *Gondwanaland*).

Pingvin. Penguin; also, a Soviet tracked vehicle by that name used in snow and ice terrain.

Pioner. Pioneer; also, a member of the Young Pioneers, the scouting and political organization for children and early teenagers.

Pleistocene (Ice Age). Geological epoch characterized by great expansion of glaciers in the Northern Hemisphere and lasting from approximately two million to ten thousand years before the present.

Polyarnaya Aviatsiya. Polar Aviation, the Soviet flying service that operates in the polar regions.

Polyarnik. A person who has made a career of working in the polar regions.

Potemkin Village. A deceptively attractive front or facade; though named for Catherine the Great's adviser Grigori A. Potemkin (1739–91), such fronts have been a standard feature of government throughout Russian history.

Pravda. Truth; name of the official journal of the Communist party of the U.S.S.R.

Purga. Snowstorm, blizzard.

Remont. Repair; reconditioning; overhaul.

Sambo. Russian form of combat sport similar to judo, emphasizing leg and foot techniques in throwing the opponent.

Samogon. Homemade or illicit alcoholic beverage; moonshine.

Samolet. Aircraft.

Sani. Sledge, sleigh.

Sastrugi. International technical term for irregular ridges formed on a snow surface by wind erosion and deposition. The axes of the ridges tend to lie at right angles to the direction of the prevailing wind. (Russian *zastrugi.*)

Seabees. Construction battalions of the U.S. Naval Civil Engineering Corps, founded in World War II. The Seabees built the U.S. bases in Antarctica for the IGY.

Sea-floor spreading. In theory, addition to and spreading apart of the oceanic crust by the upwelling of convection currents of viscous rock material along midocean ridges. New material in the sea floor moves away from the ridges at rates of one to ten centimeters per year. This mechanism drives the crustal movements described above under "new tectonics." The concept of sea-floor spreading arose from magnetometer surveys on oceanographic cruises of the late 1950s and early 1960s.

Sea ice. Any form of ice in the sea that has resulted from the freezing of seawater.

Seismic sounding. Fixing depth of a geologic structure by creating seismic waves (using explosions or other means) and analyzing the echoes reflected or refracted to the surface. In recent years, radio-echo sounding has largely replaced seismic sounding for penetrating ice sheets.

Seismograph. An instrument that records vibrations in the earth; it may be stationary, as for recording earthquakes, or portable, as when used in seismic sounding.

Seismology. The study of earthquakes and the vibrations or seismic waves they produce in the earth. Can include study of waves generated by such artificial means as explosions and of the structure of the Earth's interior, which transmits the waves.

Sever. North.

Severnaya. Northern.

Shield. A large, geologically stable part of a continent that consists of ancient rocks and has a generally subdued topography, such as the Canadian or Antarctic Shield.

Sklad. Depot, warehouse, or supply dump.

Skua. A large, powerful, predatory bird of the jaeger family; the south polar skua is common along the Antarctic coast during the austral summer and has been known to range far inland.

Solidarnost. Solidarity.

Soviets. Russian *sovet* = "council") At the time of the revolution, popularly elected bodies that sought to represent the interests of the workers and peasants; these true soviets were superseded by the party-state machine.

Soyuz. Union or federation; often used to stand for *Sovetskiy Soyuz* (Soviet Union) and occurring in words like *profsoyuz* (trade union).

Sputnik. Satellite; fellow-traveler. The first artificial earth satellite, *Sputnik-1*, was launched into orbit by the U.S.S.R. on October 4, 1957.

Synoptic. In meteorology, simultaneously existing conditions that can be observed over a broad area to give a general description of the weather as an aid to forecasting.

Tabular iceberg. A flat-topped iceberg with clifflike sides, usually calved from an ice shelf.

Taiga. The great subarctic north woods of Eurasia, largely of fir, pine, and spruce, stretching from Scandinavia to the Pacific Ocean and covering much of Siberia.

Tashkent. Islamic city of Soviet Central Asia, capital of Uzbekistan. Tashkent is situated in an oasis of the Red Sand Desert, and to Russians its name is synonymous with sweltering heat.

Tectonics. Study of the structural features of the earth's crust, their origin, historical evolution, mutual relations, and modes of deformation.

Thermodynamics. Branch of physics that deals with the nature of heat and its relation to mechanical and other forms of energy. Because of its applications in engineering, thermodynamics has been closely associated with the development of the industrial revolution, and it is relevant to many fields of scientific and technological research.

Tochka Povorota. Turning point, changing direction or heading.

Troika. Team of three horses abreast pulling a sleigh or carriage.

Tsunami. (Japanese: "harbor wave") A sea wave produced by a rapid, large-scale disturbance of the ocean floor. It is usually the result of a shallow submarine earthquake, in which case it can be called a seismic sea wave, but may also be caused by a submarine landslide or volcanic eruption. In the open sea, tsunamis travel rapidly, have very long waves and low amplitudes, and are barely noticeable, but in shallow water they slow down and pile up destructively on exposed shores. Tsunamis are often erroneously called "tidal waves."

U-2.   High-altitude, long-range reconnaissance airplane used for U.S. intelligence missions.

Uragan.   Hurricane; technically, a wind of force 12 on the Beaufort scale, with velocity over sixty-four knots (seventy-four MPH or twenty-nine meters per second).

Verkhoyansk.   A town in the taiga of northeastern Siberia; the lowest temperatures in the world outside of Antarctica are regularly recorded in its vicinity.

Veter.   Wind; breeze.

Vostochnyy.   Eastern; oriental.

Vostok.   East.

Wanigan.   Movable shelter that was used by American Indians; hence, a mobile hut mounted on a sledge, tractor, etc., for the use of a U.S. field party.

Weddell seal.   Largest and most common of the four types of Antarctic seals. The dark, lethargic Weddell, which may weigh up to half a ton, has been known to dive as deep as two thousand feet and stay under water for as long as forty minutes.

Wehrmacht.   The German armed forces in World War II.

Yolka.   Fir tree, traditionally used as a Christmas tree.

Yug.   South.

Yuzhnyy Polyus.   South pole.

Zapad.   West.

Zapadnyy.   Western.